The Newcomen Society for the Study of the History of Engineering and Technology

Extra Publication No. 7

RAILWAYS IN ENGLAND
1826 and 1827

Ueber Schienenwege in England: Bemerkungen gesammelt auf einer Reise in den Jahren 1826 und 1827

(CONCERNING RAILWAYS IN ENGLAND: OBSERVATIONS COLLECTED DURING A JOURNEY IN THE YEARS 1826 AND 1827)

BY

C. VON OEYNHAUSEN AND H. VON DECHEN

Mining Ministry Supervisory Assessors

TRANSLATED FROM THE GERMAN TEXT BY

E. A. FORWARD

EDITED BY

CHARLES E. LEE

in collaboration with

K. R. GILBERT

PUBLISHED FOR

THE NEWCOMEN SOCIETY

BY W. HEFFER AND SONS LIMITED

CAMBRIDGE

1971

ISBN 0 85270 048 2

Printed in Great Britain by W. Heffer and Sons Ltd, Cambridge

CONTENTS

FOREWORD

Much of our detailed knowledge of early industrial development in Great Britain is derived from the writings of visitors from overseas who came for the purpose of gaining information about our pioneer achievements, and were afforded facilities. After the Peace of Paris was signed on 10 February 1763, the enormous industrial progress being made in England attracted technical and engineering visitors from the Continent, and an outstanding early example is provided by the visit from July 1764 until September 1765 of Gabriel Jars of the Royal Academy of Science in Paris. His six reports[1] to the French Government between 6 May and 6 September 1765 were included by his brother in the three-volume publication *Voyages Metallurgiques* issued between 1774 and 1781. These provide an invaluable source of information at a particularly interesting period.

Wars in many parts of the world restricted the free flow of information, and later published reports of a similar kind were intermittent until after 1815, by which time there had been enormous further progress in Great Britain. A privately-financed society in Philadelphia, U.S.A., despatched William Strickland (1788–1854) to England in March 1825, accompanied by Samuel Honeyman Kneass (1806–58) as draughtsman. The *Reports on Canals, Railways, Roads, and other Subjects, made to the Pennsylvania Society for the Promotion of Internal Improvement* by William Strickland, was published in 1826; and it describes and illustrates much which might otherwise have escaped record.

Shortly after the Strickland visit, two Prussian mining engineers came to England specifically to study the railways here and made their enquiries with typical Teutonic thoroughness, even to the extent of pacing the lengths of railway inclines to satisfy themselves as to the precision of the information supplied by their informants. Their Report was published in *Archiv für Bergbau und Hüttenwesen*, vol. XIX (1829) and was issued by G. Reimer of Berlin (apparently from the same type) as a separate book, also in 1829. This is the text which forms the subject of the present translation. Although the title-page of the Report states that the journey took place in 1826 and 1827, there is little internal evidence of the precise dating of individual visits. It seems probable that the tour began in the latter part of 1826, and was completed by the summer of 1827. The few dates mentioned in the text indicate that the authors were in South Lancashire in April 1827, and on the North-East Coast in May 1827; the latter was possibly a return visit.

This Report seems to have been unknown to British writers until 1921, when the late J. G. H. Warren found a reference to it, discovered the original, and used some portions dealing with the locomotives and stationary engines of the Stockton & Darlington Railway, which were translated for him by the late Dr H. W. Dickinson. These quotations were included by Warren in his book *A Century of Locomotive Building by Robert Stephenson & Co.*, 1823–1923. The major portion of the Report remained unexplored until it was translated by the late E. A. Forward in April to July 1942 at the instigation of the late C. F. Dendy Marshall, who thought that it might be published by the

[1] See the paper on Gabriel Jars's visit to Great Britain in 1764 by M. Jean Chevalier, presented to the Newcomen Society on 10 December 1947 (*Trans.* vol. XXVI, pp. 57–68, 'La Mission de Gabriel Jars dans les Mines et les Usines Britanniques en 1764'). Gabriel Jars was born on 26 January 1732 and died on 20 August 1769.

Newcomen Society as an Extra Publication. This was impracticable at the time, partly because of labour and paper shortages during the war and its aftermath. It was then proposed that a short abstract should be prepared for publication in the *Transactions of the Newcomen Society*, so that members could be apprised of the contents of this valuable work. E. A. Forward duly prepared a Report on these lines, and presented it to the Society on 14 October 1953.[1] The translation remained unpublished, although Forward helped students of particular railways by supplying short extracts.

Ernest Alfred Forward[2] was born in London on 5 September 1877 and in 1901 entered the service of the Machinery and Inventions Division of the Victoria and Albert Museum, which became part of the Science Museum on its foundation in 1909. As an historian and a mechanical engineer, his main interest was the early development of the steam locomotive, on which subject he contributed numerous papers and articles. He was a founder member of the Newcomen Society, Treasurer from 1921 to 1931, and a Vice-President from 1936 to 1938. In 1937 he retired from the Science Museum with the rank of Keeper, but continued his studies during his retirement and gave valued assistance to other historians. He died at Croydon on 14 October 1959, aged 82. On his death the manuscript of this translation was deposited with the Newcomen Society, and eventually the present Editor was asked to examine it with a view to publication. A comparison with the German text indicated that the form of some of the translation adhered too closely to the linguistic structure of the German to permit of easy reading, and this has been modified without departing from the essential method of expression of the authors. In this task the Editor acknowledges with gratitude the constant co-operation of his wife (Cécile Kerslake Lee). Naturally, with a work written nearly a century and a half ago, problems have arisen in endeavouring to express accurately the intentions of the authors where they used words capable of bearing more than one meaning. In resolving such problems, the collaboration of Mr K. R. Gilbert has been invaluable, but he has not checked the whole text, and his responsibility is confined to the specific queries that have been submitted to him.

CHARLES E. LEE

9 *January* 1970

---

[1] *Trans.* vol. XXIX, pp. 1–12.

[2] See obituary notice in *Trans.* vol. XXXII, p. 149.

THE AUTHORS

When the authors of this report came to England in 1826, they had both secured recognition in Prussia as mineralogists and geologists, and were civil servants with the rank of Supervisory Assessor in the Mining Department of the Ministry of the Interior. At the time of their visit von Oeynhausen was 31 years old and von Dechen 26. When the report was prepared, the name 'Carl' was spelled normally with a 'C' and this initial appears on the title-page. This practice has survived in English with such names as Cologne, but, as a result of the increasing substitution of 'K' in German usage, the references to the authors in standard German biographies use 'K'.

Karl August Ludwig Freiherr von Oeynhausen was born at Grevenburg, near Höxter, in Westphalia, on 4 February 1795. He chose mining as his profession, and began his practical training in the mines of Cisleben. Then he entered the University of Göttingen, where he studied Natural Sciences and Mathematics until 1816, but with a break of some months in 1813 and 1814, when he served the Fatherland in resisting the invasion of Napoleon. In 1816 he joined the Mining Office at Waldenburg, in Silesia, and in 1817 went to Tarnowitz, in Upper Silesia. At the latter place he achieved some distinction for his geological investigations of Upper Silesia and the neighbouring territory, on which subject he published a book in 1822. After he had passed the qualifying examination for mining on 1 April 1820, he was attached to the Westphalian Mining Office, and in 1824 he was appointed Chief Mining Official in the Mining Department of the Ministry of the Interior. He travelled extensively through Germany, Northern France, the territory which became Belgium, and Great Britain, enlarging his knowledge of mining practice. After returning from Great Britain in 1827, he was appointed Technical Officer in the Head Mining Office in Berlin, and thereafter pursued a distinguished career in various parts of the country. He was at Bonn in 1828, and at Dortmund later in the same year, where he was appointed Chief Mining Councillor. As such, he went in 1830 to Halle and in 1831 to Bonn, where he remained for ten years. In 1844 he was appointed a Privy Councillor in the Finance Ministry, to which the mining works and salt works were attached. His name is associated particularly with the boring for salt at Neusalzwerk, where numerous improvements in boring tackle are attributed to him. He was instrumental in establishing the salt baths at Neusalzwerk, opened on 18 May 1845, and Friedrich Wilhelm IV recognised his work on 25 August 1845 by giving this spa the name 'Bad Oeynhausen'. In 1860 the University of Berlin conferred on von Oeynhausen a Doctorate (*honoris causa*). Ill health caused his resignation from the mining service in June 1864, and his return to his family at Gravenburg, where he died on 1 February 1865, only three days short of his seventieth birthday.

Ernst Heinrich Karl von Dechen was born in Berlin on 25 March 1800, and was educated in the University of that city. He then studied mining in Bochum and Essen, and in 1820 joined the Mining Department of the Prussian State, in which he served until 1864. Early in his career, he spent some years in travels through the important mining districts of Germany, England, and France. For his work as a university lecturer, he received the degree of Doktor (*honoris causa*). In 1841 he transferred to Bonn as Superintendent of the Mines of the Rhine Provinces, and substantial progress in mining and metallurgical works in Rhenish Prussia resulted from his activities. In the winter of 1859–60 he took over temporarily the direction of the Department of Mines, Factories, and Salt Works in the Ministry of Commerce. He retired from the State Service in 1864 with the title of Excellency, but he then had before him another quarter of a century of activity in civil government. In Bonn, he had become a Town Councillor in 1846, and he continued in office until the end of his life. Also, he was called to the Prussian Council of State in 1884. It has been stated of von Dechen that there was scarcely any large industrial undertaking in the Rhineland or Westphalia that was not indebted to him. He made considerable efforts towards improving the means of transport in mining, and also in the related activity of extending the markets for the products of mines and factories. His scientific work was basically in the sphere of geology, and his numerous contributions to geological literature extend over the period from 1825 to 1882. An outstanding work was his geological map of Rhenish Prussia and Westphalia in 35 sheets on the scale of 1:80,000, issued with two volumes of explanatory text. He died at Bonn on 15 February 1889.

Brief biographies of both authors are given in *Biographisch-Literarisches Handwörterbuch* by J. C. Poggendorff; and by Dr Conrad Matschoss (1871–1942), the German engineering historian, in *Männer der Technik*. The *Encyclopaedia Britannica* (11th edition, 1910) includes a note on von Dechen by Horace Bolingbroke Woodward of the Geological Survey of England and Wales. There are also the separate volumes *Karl von Oeynhausen* by O. Liesenhoff, Berlin, 1895; and *Heinrich von Dechen, ein Lebensbild* by Hugo Laspeyres, Bonn, 1889.

INTRODUCTION

(By the Authors)

It would be difficult to find a subject which, in recent years, has attracted so much general interest as that provided by the extensive schemes which have been, and are still being, prepared daily in England, for the improvement of inland communications. When on the one hand newspaper accounts and other reports about railways on which general traffic of all kinds of vehicles takes place, or of locomotive engines which run on ordinary roads, and of the enormous speeds with which these move, the matter becomes almost ridiculous; on the other hand there is still lacking more definite and descriptive news about these schemes. Hitherto, railways have been designed for different purposes, but chiefly to bring coal, ore, slag, and stone from the source to the destined place of use. At some places they are employed for connecting separate parts of canals, especially where great differences of level, in short distances, would have made a water connection very difficult. Hitherto there have never been railways destined solely for this purpose, which were intended to be laid on ordinary roads, among all the various traffic found on them, and that which is now being laid between Liverpool and Manchester, should certainly fulfil this aim, but only under very special conditions. On another railway which is intended chiefly for the transport of coal, limestone, and the like, there is incidentally a regular coach service.

The first use of railways in England is supposed to have been made at the collieries of Newcastle, about 1630, in order to transport the coal from the pits to the staiths on the Tyne. At that time they were built of wood, as they are at present at many mines in Germany. In the middle of the last century, when wood became dearer, and the use of cast-iron more general, these rails were made of cast-iron, and only in the past few years have wrought-iron rails been employed. Wherever a large weight of goods has to be transported regularly between two fixed points, then railways show themselves to be practicable; these circumstances occur especially at mines and then depots and at foundries. At first they were used only over small stretches of country; hills to be passed over set a limit to their use. Soon, however, it was shown to be of special advantage to allow loads from the heights to descend; complete canal boats were let down and drawn up by means of inclined railways between the parts of canals. Similar inclined planes were placed to connect nearly level railways, and so the possibility of overcoming every difficulty of the ground was offered by them. For a long time, railways had only a restricted use. For connecting more widely separated points, special systems of canals were made in England after the first, the Sankey Canal, 1755, and the Bridgewater Canal, 1758, had so completely fulfilled their purpose. Once the costly outlay was made, canal transport was very cheap—so long as a water supply was available—and also regular, excepting when winter frost is taken into consideration. At present there are about 80 canals in Great Britain. Many, however, are far from being able to pay the interest on their cost of construction, and with more than 40 the shares have only half their original value. There is a limit to the speed of the canal boats, which can be exceeded only with disproportionate expenditure of power. Besides this, the amount of the water supply sets a limit to the weight which can be transported; while the form of the country may necessitate long detours or make the laying out extraordinarily difficult. These circumstances have made it possible for railways to compete with canals, so that the scheme for a railway between Manchester and Liverpool, which already have a canal connection, is on the point of being accomplished. In general, railways are more suitable for comparison with canals (and to replace and to compensate for them), than with roads. At least until now, roads have not been replaced by canals. The form of the land restricts the layout of roads very little; they are not obliged to conform to regular divisions of ascents, descents, and horizontal levels, and they permit the general use of any kind of vehicle. Also, the maintenance of roads and transport thereon are far more costly than is the case with railways.

For a long time horses provided the only motive power employed on railways and canals; on the latter they are still used except on inclined planes, upon which steam engines and water wheels are employed as the motive power. Since the beginning of this century, steam locomotive engines have been constructed, and attempts have been made to replace horses on railways by these. However, even at the most favourable points, their applicability has not yet been sufficiently proved, and at present they are employed only under certain restricted conditions. The use of stationary steam-engines for inclines where the loads are drawn upwards, and also on the level parts of the line, has become common, and they appear to be very suitable where considerable loads must be transported over a line, and where a high speed is required.

We are strongly of the opinion that railways should take in civil engineering a far-reaching share which until now has been little cultivated. This is by reason of their objects; of the country they traverse; of the kind of layout; of the moving powers and their effects; of their cost of construction and maintenance, and of their whole economic aims.

Two of the most remarkable railways in the north of England, the so-called Darlington Railway from Bishop Auckland to Stockton on Tees, and the Hetton Railway from the Colliery of the same name to Sunderland on the Wear, must be cited as examples, the former of a wrought-iron, and the latter of a cast-iron railway. Inclined planes with stationary steam-engines; self-acting planes, where the full wagons descending draw up the empty ones; stationary steam-engines which effect the haulage on nearly horizontal stretches of line; locomotive engines;—all present themselves in this connection.

Then further remarks will be made about some other railways in England, Wales, and Scotland; about inclined planes which are connected with canals; and about special and distinctive methods of constructing railways and their applicability.

Finally, several matters will be discussed with regard to their plans and effects, the chief aim of which will be to answer the question as to what conditions in the laying out of railways are practicable and suitable for the end in view.

So many and so varied are the circumstances concerned that a comprehensive general statement would be difficult to express, and in every case a special comparison of all concurrent conditions is necessary. Meanwhile, it is always possible to explain this by statements of experience and surveys. A private individual, when he makes such a plan, must take entirely different considerations into account from those which affect the State, when it considers it advisable to undertake such a work in order to attain higher or more extensive aims. The first must keep to a close estimate of the expected profits, or he must make certain of covering any loss by the predominant profits in other branches of his business; he must calculate the interest on the business capital at so high a rate that he can repay the capital by degrees therefrom. The State, on the other hand, must place this outlay in the category of that which repays itself by indirect advantages, through the enlivenment of industry, and of internal communications, through the increase of the national wealth, but not through direct revenue. When a private owner collects a toll for the use of a railway, this must amply cover all interest and running costs. However, when the State imposes such a toll, only the running costs, and those of maintenance, administration, etc., need be met by this income.

As matters now stand, it would seldom be the case that the State would take such a general interest in a railway as to give a considerable interest-free capital to the scheme. Such arrangements are more suited to raising the production of single works or establishments than to influence the common trade of whole districts. However, such cases can occur, if it is shown that railways provide a regular connection more effectively than canals, which need sufficient water, or than making navigable rivers with steep descents. The smaller cost of construction of the railway could assure a more moderate freight charge at all times than can be achieved upon the waterways.

COMPARISON OF THE ENGLISH AND PRUSSIAN WEIGHTS AND MEASURES

Since, in the descriptions, it is sometimes necessary to introduce English weights and measures, it is desirable to give here a short comparison of these with the Prussian weights and measures.

1 foot Engl. = 0·97113 foot Pruss.
= 11·65356 in. Pruss.
1 foot Pruss. = 1·029728 feet Engl.
1 yard = 3 feet Engl. = 2·91339 feet Pruss.
= 34·9606 in. Pruss.
= 0·437007 fathoms of 80 in. Pruss.
1 fathom = 6 feet Engl. = 5·82678 feet Pruss.
= 69·9212 in. Pruss.
= 0·874015 fathoms Pruss.
1 fathom Pruss. (lachter) = 2·288290 yards = 1·144145 fathoms Engl.
1 chain = 22 yards = 63·09458 feet Pruss.
= 9·614165 fathoms Pruss.
= 5·25788 poles Pruss.
1 furlong = 10 chains = 630·9458 feet Pruss.
= 96·14165 fathoms Pruss.
= 52·5788 poles Pruss.
1 mile = 8 furlongs = 5,280 feet Engl. = 5,047·5664 feet Pruss.
= 769·1332 fathoms Pruss.
= 420·6304 poles Pruss.
= 0·2103152 miles Pruss.
1 mile Pruss. = 4·75674 miles Engl.
1 square yard = 1,222·067326 square inches Pruss.
= 8·486578 square feet Pruss.
= 0·0589345 square poles Pruss.
1 acre = 4,840 sq. yd. = 285·24298 sq. poles Pruss.
1 lb. Avoirdupois = 0·9665577 lb. Pruss.
112 lb. = 1 cwt. = 108·25446 lb. Pruss.
= 0·984131 cwt. (Centner) Pruss.
20 cwt. = 1 ton = 2,165·0892 lb. Pruss.
= 19·68262 cwt. (Centner) Pruss.
53 cwt. = 1 Newcastle chaldron = 52·1589 cwt. (Centner) Pruss.

84 lb. = 1 bushel coal = 81·19084 lb. Pruss.
= 0·738098 cwt. (Centner) Pruss.

1 lb. Imperial Standard = 1·0519344 lb. Pruss.

1 *ton Pruss.* = 4 *cwt.* (*Centner*) *Pruss.*[1]

Prussian Coinage in 1827

(*These figures were obtained by the translator from comparisons in various parts of the book*)

1 Reichsthaler = 30 groschen = 360 pfennige
= 34·3 pence Engl.

1 grs. = 1·1433 pence Engl.

10 grs. = 11·433 pence Engl.

Approximately 10 grs. = 12 pence = 120 pfg.

1 penny Engl. = 10 pfg.

£1 is reckoned at 7 thalers in Berlin.

[1] *This item is not shown in the table given by the authors. It is taken by the translator from the calculations in connection with the Hetton Colliery Railway* (*p.* 33).—*Ed.*

WROUGHT-IRON RAILWAY AT DARLINGTON IN THE COUNTY OF DURHAM

General Observations

At Darlington, in the County of Durham, a railway more than 31 English miles long (6½ miles Pruss.) was planned in 1822 and finished in 1825.[1] This railway is at present unquestionably the best in Great Britain; it will soon be surpassed, however, by the new Liverpool & Manchester Railway, a great and practical undertaking which is now being built. Also, this great railway is being constructed on essentially the same principles as those adopted at Darlington, and by the same engineer, Mr G. Stephenson of Newcastle.

The chief aim of the Darlington Railway is the transport of coal from the collieries near Auckland to the shipping places on the River Tees at Stockton.

In addition to this, the railway conveys a large quantity of quicklime, as well as all kinds of goods.

Although the main line and several branch lines are completed, yet more branches are being planned, and by these the transport on the main line will be increased and improved considerably. In addition to the goods wagons, many coaches go daily on this railway from Auckland to Stockton, and back. These coaches, provided with one horse, can transport from 50 to 60 persons. The journey from Darlington to Stockton, a distance of 12 miles (2½ miles Pruss.) occupies 70 minutes, and for each English mile the passenger pays 1 penny (⅚ grs. Pruss.). Thus, from Darlington to Stockton the passenger pays one shilling (10 grs. Pruss.). The charge for a Prussian mile, which takes 28 minutes, is therefore 4 grs.[2]

The laying out of this railway, on which, for the first time, wrought-iron rails in quantity were employed, was undertaken by a joint-stock company (of which Mr Pease of Darlington is the chief shareholder) and was completed in 4 years. This company was authorised by an Act of Parliament. The capital which the company has up to now (at the end of 1826) expended is said to amount to £167,000 sterling (1,169,000 thl.). Of this, about £35,000 (245,000 thl.) had to be paid for land purchase, sometimes at £600 (4,200 thl.) per acre. This capital includes several expenses which are connected with the railway only indirectly, such as about £4,000 (28,000 thl.) which the first appeal to Parliament cost, in order to overcome the opposition which ranged itself against the railway scheme; further for the building of several inns along the line of the railway; as well as a very considerable expense for trials and the cost of alterations and improvements that had been adopted.

Despite this large outlay, the undertaking promises to be a very great success. At present, the monthly nett takings amount to between £1,500 to £1,800 (10,500 to 12,600 thl.) or about £20,000

---

[1] *The Stockton & Darlington Railway Company was incorporated by an Act of* 19 *April* 1821 (1 & 2 *Geo. IV, cap.* 44). *It was opened on* 27 *September* 1825.—*Ed.*

[2] The interchange of coaches between Darlington and Stockton gives a striking demonstration of how much communication increases when the means of communication are made simpler and better. Before the making of the railway, only two coaches went weekly between Darlington and Stockton, and these were often almost empty. At present, at least three coaches daily traverse the route, each laden with 50 to 60 persons, so that, whereas formerly only 20 persons made use of the coaches weekly, now 350 persons weekly are transported along the railway and likewise back again, while, by reason of the very low fare, nobody goes on foot any longer, or makes use of any other, more expensive, means. (*Footnote by Authors.*)

(140,000 thl.) yearly, which would pay interest of nearly 12 per cent on the capital, and in all probability these takings will become considerably greater in the future.

In the Act of Parliament which authorised the company, fines were laid down by means of which order and security will be preserved on the railway. They are as follow:—

Extract from the Act of Parliament in the second year of George IV, concerning the before-named railway.

(1) Everyone who neglects or refuses to give to the tollkeeper a written statement of the quantity of goods or other objects in the wagon or other vehicle, a written proof of their origin and destination, or refuses to show a waybill or who imparts wrong information, or who consigns or delivers any part of the load to another point than is shown on the bill of lading, incurs a fine of not more than .. .. 10 shillings.

(2) Whoever rides, leads, or drives a horse, mule, donkey, cow, or any other cattle on to the railway or on to any place belonging thereto, incurs a fine of not more than .. .. £2.

(3) Everyone who passes across this railway with a wagon or other vehicle which is not constructed specially for the way, with the exception of the possessor of the adjacent land; or on a public or private road, incurs a fine of not more than .. .. £5.

(4) Every owner of a wagon who neglects to register his name and address and the number of his wagon or vehicle with the clerk of the company, and who neglects to paint on it the name and number in white letters at least 3 in. high on a back ground, or who refuses to allow the wagon to be gauged or measured at the expense of the company, incurs a fine not exceeding.. £5.

(5) Damage of any kind which is caused to the railway, or to the material going along it, or to the adjacent land, by any wagon or other vehicle, or by the wagon driver or other person belonging to it, when such damage does not exceed £20, the author of the same shall repay the amount of the damage, and in addition, shall incur a fine not exceeding .. .. .. £2.

(6) Whoever neglects to shut gates made over the railway through which he has passed, incurs a fine not exceeding .. .. £2.

(7) Every yard inspector who gives anyone priority in the loading or unloading of wagons incurs a fine not exceeding .. .. £2.

(8) Whoever leaves a wagon standing on the railway and thereby obstructs the way, if he refuses to remove it when requested to do so, incurs a fine of not over .. .. 5 shillings.

(9) Whoever trespasses on the railway, and demolishes or destroys any part of it, or steals anything from it, incurs the same punishment as that incurred for a felony.

(10) Tollkeepers who demand or raise a larger toll than that set down by the company, incur a fine not over .. .. £5.

Fines fixed by the Bye-laws of the Railway Company; brought into operation 11 *July* 1826

(1) Every attendant who leaves unattended his horse, wagon, or locomotive engine, which travel on the railway, incurs a fine not over .. .. 10 shillings.

(2) Every attendant who, at the request of a shareholder, agent, or official of the railway company, refuses to give his baptismal and family names, his place of abode or the name of his master, incurs a fine, not exceeding .. .. £2.

(3) Everyone who draws away a wagon except by the special turnout points, incurs a fine not over .. .. £5.

(4) Everyone who goes over the railway one hour before sunrise or later than one hour after sunset, without written permission from the company or its agent, incurs a fine, not over .. £2.

(5) Every wagon driver or owner of wagons, of which the track width does not measure 4 ft 5½ in. from the outside of the wheelrims, the breadth of the wheels 3 in., and the distance centre to centre 4 ft incurs a fine, not over .. .. 5 shillings.
(N.B. The distance of the axles is, however, only 38½ in. Rheinl.)

(6) Every wagon driver or owner who does not have a suitable brake, with which to regulate the speed, incurs a fine of not over .. .. £2.

(7) Every wagon driver who allows coal, stone, or other material, which fall from his wagon, to remain lying on the railway; and thereby obstruct the line, incurs a fine not over .. £2.

(8) Every wagon driver, who does not at once inform an official of the company, when a wagon passing along the railway has broken or displaced a rail, incurs a fine not over .. £2.

(9) Everyone who refuses to deposit, in the place appointed by the depot overseer, goods or merchandise which ought to be unloaded from a ship, wagon, or other vehicle at a depot of the company, must bear the cost of any damage arising out of such refusal, and in addition incurs a fine not over .. .. £2.

(10) Every proprietor of coal, line, minerals, lead, goods, or merchandise, who leaves these on the railway for too long a time, so that the haulage is hindered, must compensate the company for the cost of removing them.

(11) Every agent or toll collector who is either an owner or part owner of wagons or horses which pass over the railway, or the merchants or traders in beverages, foodstuffs, and goods of other kinds put on the railway, without written permission of the committee or sub-committee, incur a fine not over .. .. £5.

(12) Everyone who travels with empty wagons on the railway, and refuses to take to the siding when loaded wagons approach, incurs a fine of not over .. .. 10 shillings

(13) Everyone who refuses to take to the siding when a locomotive engine approaches, incurs a fine of not over .. .. 10 shillings.

(14) Every attendant of a locomotive engine who allows anyone at all, apart from the assistants or agents of the company, to travel on the engine or wagons connected with it, incurs a fine of not over .. .. 10 shillings.

(15) Every engine attendant, vehicle or wagon driver, who leaves the coupling chains or bars of the wagons anywhere on the railway, except in the depots or at the foot of the eastern slope of the Brusselton incline, incurs a fine of not over .. .. 10 shillings.

(16) Every engine attendant, vehicle or wagon driver, who carries coal, good, or other materials in the company's wagons, and neglects to lubricate the axles of these wagons properly, incurs a fine of not over .. .. £1.

(17) Everyone, apart from the agents and servants of the company, who travels on a wagon or locomotive engine on the railway, without permission of the company or its agents, incurs a fine of not over .. .. 10 shillings.

(18) Every engine attendant or wagon driver who neglects to inform the company or its agents

when a wagon or vehicle collides with something on the railway, incurs a fine of not over .. .. 10 shillings.

(19) Every engine attendant or wagon driver who neglects to put the wedge in the points in the position corresponding with the main line, incurs a fine of not above .. .. .. £1.

(20) Every engine attendant or wagon driver who takes to the siding and neglects to place the wedge in the points so that the wagons can follow down the side line, incurs a fine of not more than .. .. £1.

(21) Everyone who puts coal, stone, lime, wood, or other materials on the railway, or on the side path of the same, incurs a fine of not over .. .. £1.

(22) Every agent or servant of the company who neglects immediately to inform the sub-committee or one of the clerks of the company, of the infringement of one of the above regulations, when such comes to his notice, incurs a fine of not over .. .. 10 shillings.

(23) Every owner or driver of a wagon on the railway, which is used for the transport of passengers, who refuses to follow the directions and rules of the company, its committee or sub-committee, regarding the departure of coaches or other vehicles from Darlington, Stockton, or any other point on the line, or the positioning of any coach or other vehicle, or who acts against these rules, incurs a fine of not over .. .. £2.

(24) Every proprietor or driver of a coach or other vehicle intended for the transport of passengers on the railway, who, with the exception of the passenger's effects, takes on other parcels or baggage weighing more than 28 lb, incurs a fine of not over .. .. £2.

Regulations concerning taking to the Sidings

(1) When a train of loaded wagons going down the line meet another loaded train coming up the line, the first takes to the siding, except when the wagons meet between the sidings; in this case the loaded wagons going up are taken back, down the line, to the nearest siding.
(2) All empty wagons going up or down take to the nearest siding, when they meet loaded wagons.
(3) Locomotive engines need not take to the sidings, except when meeting one another, in which case the empty train takes to the siding.
(4) A passenger coach need not take to the siding, except when it meets a locomotive engine or a train of loaded wagons.
(5) For the infringement of these rules, a fine is incurred, not exceeding .. 10 shillings.

A great part of the coal is exported from Stockton by ships on the River Tees. At present, however, the journey on this river is still very imperfect, since only ships of from 150 to 160 tons (tons of 20 cwt) lading can reach Stockton. In order to improve the shipment, the railway must be continued a further 6 miles ($1\frac{1}{4}$ miles Pruss.) down the river to where ships of more than 300 tons lading can reach, as here the depth of the water at high tide amounts to 18 ft. However, in order to lengthen the railway, the River Tees must be crossed by a bridge, which cannot be effected without considerable expense.

General description of the Railway: Its Length

The railway consists of a main line and several branches, some of which lead to different collieries and others to different depots. At present the company is constantly occupied with laying out new branch lines, both to improve and to increase the traffic. The present length of the railway is given in the following statement:—

(1) The main line	24 miles	5 furlongs	3 chains
(2) Blackboy branch	2 miles	5 furlongs	4 chains
(3) Darlington branch	—	5 furlongs	2 chains
(4) Croft branch	3 miles	3 furlongs	—
Total	31 miles	2 furlongs	9 chains

A length of 24,029 fathoms Pruss.

These figures omit the Yarm branch, the length of which is inconsiderable.

Collieries, Limestone Quarries

The chief reason for the planning of this railway was to secure a larger sale for the coal district of Auckland, which lies in the southwest part of the County of Durham. The most important collieries which send coal along this railway are, Witton Park, Etherley, West Auckland, and Old Blackboy. They lie in a group above and west of Darlington; the most distant about 13 miles ($2\frac{3}{4}$ miles Pruss.). The limestone quarries lie about 2 or 3 miles above Darlington, directly on the main line; it is a limestone belonging to the formation known as magnesian, which forms a layer 30 ft thick immediately over the coal beds, and in this the quarries are cut. The limekilns are built close by the main line; the lime is used preferably to manure the fields, and forms an important article of transport.

A very fortunate circumstance for the transport of both coal and lime is that their course is directed from the higher to the lower points, on which account proportionately inconsiderable loads are moved in the opposite direction.

Inclines on the Railway

The railway (the main line) has to surmount two hill ridges at its upper or western end, which it does by means of inclined planes over which the wagons are drawn by fixed steam-engines. These engines are erected near Greenfield and Brusselton, on the tops of both ridges. The former, the more westerly, engine is of 30 horsepower, and the latter of 60 horsepower, because here a greater number of wagons has to be transported.

At the Greenfield engine the height of the inclined plane is:—

(*a*) the north side	. .	100 ft English
(*b*) the south side	. .	$214\frac{1}{2}$,, ,,

At the Brusselton engine, however:—

(*a*) on the west side	. .	165 ft 9 in.
(*b*) on the east side	. .	81 ft[1]

From the last inclined plane at Brusselton to the depot at Stockton, the main line is about 20 miles ($4\frac{1}{5}$ miles Pruss.) long and has a gentle fall of 395 ft. This descent, however, is not entirely uniform, but is so arranged that the empty wagons can be drawn upwards without difficulty; at many places above Darlington the full wagons run down by their own weight, and must even be braked somewhat.

[1] These inclined planes are also called Etherley north and south inclined planes, and Brusselton west and east planes, and the heights of these are given as follow on the plan of the railway scheme made in 1822:—

Etherley north inclined plane	179 ft 9 in. English
,, south ,, ,,	312 ft 6 in. ,,
Brusselton east (*sic*) inclined plane	152 ft 8 in. ,,
,, west ,, ,, ,,	89 ft 8 in. ,,

These estimates, however, are not so accurate as the actual figures communicated above. (*Footnote by Authors.*)

On a short stretch the line is horizontal, and at most places below Darlington the incline is so slight that the loaded wagons will not run down by themselves.

From the following table, which has been given to us by Mr Storey, the first overseer of the railway, the rise and fall of the main line may be seen more clearly. Some divergence may have arisen through the placing of the earthworks. The table begins at the Witton Park Colliery and ends at Stockton.

Table of Inclines, Stockton & Darlington Railway

Yards of 3 ft English	Ascent	Descent	Ascent in feet	Descent in feet	Angle of ascent	Angle of descent
722	—	$\frac{1}{495}$	—	4·38		1°. 6′.56″
1,109	$\frac{1}{33}$	—	100·83	—	0°.44′.11″ Greenfield stationary steam-engine	
2,185	—	$\frac{1}{30\frac{3}{4}}$	—	213·13		1°.51′.49″
1,346	—	$\frac{1}{176}$	—	23·60		0°.19′.32″
624	—	$\frac{1}{576}$	—	83·25		0°. 5′.58″
1,851	$\frac{1}{33\frac{1}{2}}$	—	167·25	—	1°.42′.38″ Brusselton stationary steam-engine	
825	—	$\frac{1}{30\frac{1}{2}}$	—	81·15		1°.52′.58″
1,815	—	$\frac{1}{144}$	—	37·81		0°.23′.52°
2,551	—	$\frac{1}{128}$	—	59·80		0°.26′.51″
3,966	—	$\frac{1}{528}$	—	23·47		0°. 6′.31″
1,764	—	$\frac{1}{352}$	—	15·32		0°. 9′.46″
3,102	—	$\frac{1}{105}$	—	88·63		0°.32′.42°
353	—	$\frac{1}{394\frac{1}{3}}$	—	2·68		0°. 8′.43″
3,084	—	$\frac{1}{1584}$	—	5·84		0°. 2′.10″
2,876	—	$\frac{1}{1408}$	—	6·13		0°. 2′.26″
2,847	—	$\frac{1}{204\frac{1}{2}}$	—	41·76		0°.16′.48″
396	—	$\frac{1}{913}$	—	1·30		0°. 3′.46″
3,685	—	$\frac{1}{2112}$	—	5·24		0°. 1′.37″
2,205	—	$\frac{1}{253}$	—	26·15		0°.13′.35″
44	—	—	—	—	—	—

Yards of 3 ft English	Ascent	Descent	Ascent in feet	Descent in feet	Angle of ascent	Angle of descent
1,427	—	$\frac{1}{226}$	—	19·00		0°.15′.13″
88	—	$\frac{1}{478}$	—	0·55		0°. 7′.12″
1,408	—	$\frac{1}{1584}$	—	2·74		0°. 2′.10″
2,042	—	$\frac{1}{104}$	—	58·80		0°.33′. 3″
33,653	—	$\frac{1}{255\frac{1}{2}}$	—	395·22 ft fall from the last inclined plane at Brusselton		0°.13′.27″
42,315 yards whole length of the main line = 42 m,[1] o f., 3½ ch.						

[1] *The figure appears in the German text as '42 m.' but is obviously a transposition by the printer, and should read 24 m.—(Translator's footnote.)*

This table shows that, from the last inclined plane, for a total length of 33,653 yards (or 19·12 miles), the main line has a very gentle fall of 395·22 ft, a fall which amounts over the whole length to $\frac{1}{255\frac{1}{2}}$, or an angle of 0°.13′.27″.

From the beginning of the line at Witton Park to the eastern foot of the Brusselton inclined plane there is a fall of 137·43 ft on a length of 8,662 yards, or $\frac{1}{189}$ = 0°.18′.11″. If tunnels had been driven through both these hill ridges, a length of approximately 6,000 yards or 2,622 fathoms Pruss. would have been achieved, and the average slope of the line would have been 0°.18′.11″, so that no stationary steam-engines would have been required.

General Construction of the Railway

In general, the country over which this railway had to be made was advantageous to the work, and therefore substantial earthworks are comparatively few. In the part from Darlington to Stockton, where the fall is gentle and uniform, the line of the railway follows mostly the natural surface of the ground. Above Darlington, however, there are important earthworks, made partly by cuttings through the small hill ridges, and partly by throwing up firm embankments to fill hollows. Nevertheless, the greatest elevations, as well as the deepest cuttings, do not exceed 24 to 30 ft, and these are only on short stretches. In one swampy place, especially, from the foot of the Etherley ridge, where a bank 40 ft high had to be thrown up, this work was carried out with much difficulty, as the swampy ground was not able to support the weight of the embankment, which continually, sank and caused the ground to swell up at both sides. This difficulty is not yet removed completely, despite repeated filling up of the embankment; even the driving of ingenious pile work has met with only moderate success.

Where the line of the railway cuts into the surface of the ground, or where embankments are thrown up in order to pass over hollows, in those places where roads or footways cross the line, either over or under it, the passage is accomplished by means of masonry arches.

Where brooks had to be crossed, the railway was taken over them by arched bridges.

The rails are made of rolled wrought-iron, and the railway consists of a single line of 4 ft 6 in. Engl.

(4 ft 4·44 in. Pruss.) gauge.[1] Footways are provided on both sides of the line, so that the whole width of the way, at the upper surface, amounts normally to about 9 ft Engl.; yet this differs in different places, being sometimes larger and sometimes smaller. At intervals, sidings or passing places are built. One such siding is about 340 to 400 ft long, so that a locomotive engine with 16 to 20 wagons can be accommodated. In the regulations for the control of traffic on this railway, already mentioned, the manner in which the sidings are used is set forth, specifying how the movable switches must be kept open or closed. On the part of the railway above Darlington, there are proportionately fewer sidings than on the lower part. We counted here 12 to 14 passing places in a distance of 4 miles; in two miles near the middle of the railway there were seven sidings. The distance between the passing places is very varied. They are arranged according to the nature of the ground, etc., but effort is made to secure that from one passing place the next two must always be seen clearly. The length of the whole line is in the proportion of $3\frac{4}{7}$:1 to the length of the passing places, or the passing places amount to 28 per cent of the whole length of the railway.

The inclined planes at Greenfield and Brusselton are generally constructed with as uniform a slope as possible. This cannot be maintained exactly, but the variation is unimportant. It is more important to lessen the slope gradually at the lower end, and to allow it to run into the horizontal gently. It is equally important to lay the railway horizontally on a suitable stretch on the top of the ridge between the two inclined planes. Therefore, where the two steam-engines stand, the railway is horizontal for a length of about 300 to 360 ft, and it is laid double in order to facilitate the exchange of wagons.

On the inclined planes themselves, there is only a single line, as on them there is only one-way traffic.

The lines on the inclined planes are not straight, but make several turns, as the local conditions necessitate. The rope by which the wagons are drawn up or let down runs over guiding sheaves by which any desired turn may be negotiated with ease, provided that it is not too abrupt.

The guiding sheaves stand in the middle of the track about 24 ft apart, and the number of them on the long inclined planes is therefore considerable.

The shortest of the inclined planes is 825 yards, and the longest 2,185 yards. In order to indicate to the stationary-engine attendant at these considerable distances when the train ought to start, a tall signal post is used, at the top of which a disc is turned in an appointed direction. As it is difficult to see these signals at so great a distance, a telescope, continually pointed towards them, is placed beside the seat of the engine attendant, and through this he must look from time to time. When it is not possible to see the signals from the engine house, then long pulling-wires must be employed, but this presents no difficulty.

List of Tolls for the Stockton & Darlington Railway

For all coal, coke, coal dust, cinders, stone, marl, lime, clay, ironstone, and other material, building stone, paving stone, bricks, tiles, roof slates, and all other mine and rough articles, which are not included under another heading, building material, lead in blocks or sheets, dung, mixed manures, and all other kinds of manure. Three-halfpence per ton per mile (Engl. mile 1 grs. 3 pfg.).

For wrought-iron, cast-iron, building timber, planks, and agricultural products. Two pence per ton per mile (1 grs. 8 pfg.).

For all merchandise and wares. Two pence halfpenny per ton per mile (2 grs. 1 pfg.).

For all the above-named articles which pass a stationary steam-engine on the inclined planes of the railway. Sixpence per ton per mile for each engine (5 grs.).

[1] *This seems to be an error in the German text and should be* 4 *ft* 6 *in. Pruss.* (4 *ft* 7·6 *in. English*).—*Translator's footnote.*

For all coals or stones which are to be shipped from the harbour at Stockton on Tees. One halfpenny per ton per mile (5 pfg.).

For all lime which goes to Stockton for the same purpose. One penny per ton per mile (10 pfg.).

For the apparatus and the use of the company's wagons, in all cases. One halfpenny per ton per mile (5 pfg.).

The freight charges for the goods to be transported on the railway may be seen from the foregoing list. It follows from this that, for those coals and stone which go to Stockton to be shipped, the railway company does not at present receive more freightage than it pays to the horse drivers. This is arranged in order to increase and favour the shipment at Stockton, which is still new; this market was not counted on when the railway was built.[1] When the shipping from Stockton is suitably established, the freight charges probably will be raised.

The following table gives a summary of the charges for coal and lime to different points on the railway. From Darlington to the most distant collieries is about 13 miles (2¾ miles Pruss.); from Darlington to Yarm 9½ miles (2 miles Pruss.); and from Yarm to Stockton 4½ miles (1 mile Pruss.). The coals from Witton Park and Etherley collieries have to pass over two hill ridges upon the four inclined planes. West Auckland and Old Blackboy collieries have only two inclined planes to pass over; in future, when the new Blackboy branch is completed, the latter will have to pass over no inclined planes. Eldon and Coundon Collieries, as well as all limestone, have likewise no inclined planes to pass over.

Charges for a ton of coal and lime to different points on the Stockton–Darlington Railway

1. Coal

	To Darlington					To Yarm					To Stockton				
	Shillings	Pence	Thaler	Groschen	Pfennige	Shillings	Pence	Thaler	Groschen	Pfennige	Shillings	Pence	Thaler	Groschen	Pfennige
Witton Park	9.	–	3.	4.	6	10.	6	3.	15.	–	11.	–	3.	25.	6
Etherley	9.	–	3.	4.	6	10.	6	3.	15.	–	11.	–	3.	25.	6
do. small	4.	9	1.	20.	–	6.	3	2.	5.	6	6.	9	2.	10.	9
do. small (of large nuts)	6.	0	2.	3.	–	7.	6	2.	13.	6	8.	–	2.	24.	–
West Auckland	8.	–	2.	24.	–	9.	6	3.	9.	9	10.	–	3.	9.	3
do. small	4.	8	1.	17.	3	6.	–	2.	3.	–	6.	–	2.	3.	–
do. small (of large nuts)	5.	6	1.	27.	9	7.	6	2.	13.	6	7.	10	2.	17.	0
Old Blackboy	8.	–	2.	24.	–	9.	6	3.	9.	9	10.	0	3.	9.	3
do. small	4.	6	1.	17.	3	6.	3	2.	5.	6	6.	6	2.	8.	3
Eldon fire	7.	6	2.	13.	6	9.	–	3.	4.	6	9.	6	3.	9.	9
do. limecoal	6.	6	2.	3.	–	8.	–	2.	24.	–	8.	6	2.	29.	3
Coundon	8.	–	2.	24.	–	9.	–	3.	4.	6	10.	–	3.	9.	3
do. limecoal	6.	6	2.	3.	–	8.	–	2.	24.	–	8.	6	2.	29.	3

[1] Before the railway was built, no coal at all was shipped from Stockton. At present, this market is becoming very important, providing an additional proof of how the exchange of goods increases when a favourable opportunity occurs. (*Footnote by Authors.*)

2. Lime

	To Darlington					To Yarm					To Stockton				
	Shillings	Pence	Thaler	Groschen	Pfennige	Shillings	Pence	Thaler	Groschen	Pfennige	Shillings	Pence	Thaler	Groschen	Pfennige
Thickley	7.	6	2.	13.	6	9.	6	3.	9.	9	10.	–	3.	9.	3
Middridge	7.	6	2.	13.	6	9.	6	3.	9.	9	10.	–	3.	9.	3
Aycliffe	8.	–	2.	24.	–	10.	6	3.	15.	–	10.	10	3.	23.	10

Repair of the Railway

The repair of the railway is put out to contract; with the exception of the four inclined planes, £40 (280 thl.) is paid yearly per mile ($\frac{1}{5}$ mile Pruss.), and the necessary material is supplied by the company. On the inclined planes, likewise, the repair is given out to contract, with the exception of the guiding sheaves, which are maintained by the company. These sheaves suffer considerable wear, and therefore occasion substantial expense. The ropes with which the haulage is performed on the inclined planes are from $1\frac{1}{2}$ to $1\frac{5}{8}$ in. in diameter. They last well; a rope which was placed in use in June 1826 we found to be still in very good condition in May 1827.

Transport on the Railway

On this railway transport is effected partly with horses and partly with steam locomotive engines; five locomotive engines are in operation, and a sixth serves as reserve. On the inclined planes the wagons are drawn up by stationary steam-engines.

(*a*) *Transport by Horses*

Normally, one horse draws four wagons of coal; one such wagon holds a Newcastle chaldron (53 cwt) of coal, yet, by heaping up the load, it will perhaps hold 60 cwt. Its own weight is from 18 to 20 cwt, or in the mean 19 cwt, therefore the four wagons together weigh from 72 to 80 cwt. Four laden wagons weigh therefore 288 to 320 cwt, and this is the usual load for one horse on the downward journey, although one horse can draw as many as six wagons.

We saw one horse draw six wagons loaded with lime. The weight of such a loaded wagon, including its own weight of 19 cwt, amounts to some $63\frac{1}{2}$ cwt. (The load of a lime wagon at its maximum is 58 cwt.)

Reckoning the weight at $63\frac{1}{2}$ cwt, the burden of the horse, inclusive of the six wagons, was $6 \times 63\frac{1}{2} = 381$ cwt, of which the effective load was $6 \times 44\frac{1}{2} = 267$ cwt.

On the average, therefore, it may be taken that, on the level or on a descent of 1 in 104—33 min. angle, a horse is able to draw four loaded wagons, weighing together 300 cwt, of which 220 cwt is to be considered the true load. Uphill, and certainly on an ascent of 33 minutes, the same horse draws four empty wagons, together weighing 72 to 80 cwt.

The average speed of a good horse can be taken as not less than 3 ft (Engl.) a second, according to which one English mile would be covered in 1,760 seconds or $29\frac{1}{3}$ minutes. Taking into consideration the stops in the passing places, and for the attachment of the wagons and unloading, 35 min. for a mile can, however, be reckoned, whereby 2 hr 46 min. would be required to cover a Prussian mile.

The price of an ordinary coal wagon of one chaldron capacity is £24–£28 (168 to 196 thl.). The four wheels weigh 20 stones of 14 lb = 280 lb each; the lightest, however, weigh on average only $1\frac{1}{4}$ cwt = 140 lb. A set of four such wheels costs about £9 (63 thl.). The body of the coal wagon is made of wood, but the lime wagon is of iron plate, because the lime is loaded before it is quite cooled.

Most of the wagons belong to the railway company, and are hired out to those who send their goods by the railway. The horses belong to the drivers themselves. These drivers are in the service of the company, and receive one halfpenny (10 pfg.) for taking a ton of 20 cwt for one mile.

To ascertain the loading, weigh-houses are built at different points along the railway, and at these the loaded wagons are weighed. The weighing machines used here are similar to those employed on roads for weighing heavy goods wagons. The weight of the empty wagon, together with a number, is given on every wagon.

(b) Transport by Steam Locomotive Engines

The company is at present in possession of six steam locomotive engines. Four of them have two cylinders of 9 in. (Engl.) diameter. In all cases the stroke is 24 in. (Engl.). The usual pressure of the steam is 52 lb per sq. in., and such an engine will exercise 10 horsepower. The power of the engine corresponding to the cylinder diameter and the given pressure should amount to 15 horsepower.

In winter, or when the rails are wet, a locomotive engine usually draws 16 wagons; but in summer, when the rails are dry, 20 wagons. A wagon holds one chaldron of coal.[1] This gives a load:—

(1) The 16 to 20 empty wagons	320 to 400 cwt
(2) The 16 to 20 chaldrons of coal	848 to 1,060 cwt
Total	1,168 to 1,460 cwt

This would be the work of four to five horses; yet the engine can draw 24 wagons easily. Moreover, the speed is greater. In places where, on account of the fall of the railway, the engine has nothing to draw, its speed reaches 10 miles (Engl.) an hour ($2\frac{1}{10}$ miles Pruss.); on the average its speed is 5 miles an hour, or 7·3 ft (Engl.) a second, thus, at least double as much as that of a draft-horse; the effect of the locomotive engine is therefore equal to 8 to 10 horsepower. The journey to Stockton and back, a total distance of 40 miles (Engl.) ($8\frac{1}{2}$ miles Pruss.), is accomplished in 9 to 11 hours, according to the speed at which the loading and unloading, the shunting, etc., takes place. In case of necessity, the locomotive engine can complete two such journeys in one day and cover a distance of 80 miles (17 miles Pruss.). On the upward journey, with empty wagons, 5 miles an hour is considered a good speed.

Six wells, of which two are at the ends of the railway (that is to say, of the gently falling part, for the locomotive engines are not able to go on the inclined planes) provide the same with water. On a journey to Stockton and back (40 miles), $1\frac{1}{4}$ to $1\frac{1}{2}$ tons (25 to 30 cwt) of coal are burned. This coal is carried in a separate wagon immediately following the engine.

The weight of a locomotive engine of 10 horsepower amounts to about 132 cwt; the weight of the water contained in it is 20 cwt,[2] and the weight of the tender together with the coal is 40 cwt. In addition to its load of 1,168 to 1,460 cwt, the locomotive engine has therefore to draw a dead load of 132+20+40 = 192 cwt, or in round numbers 200 cwt.

[1] *The weight of a chaldron varied from one part of the country to another. The Newcastle chaldron (to which the authors are here referring) was declared to be 53 cwt by Statute 6 & 7 William III, cap. 10.—Ed.*

[2] *In 'A Century of Locomotive Building by Robert Stephenson & Co., 1823–1923', the late J. G. H. Warren commented (page 115) 'this is an understatement. The water must have been about 30 cwt; the engine, in working order, at least 8 tons.'—Ed.*

The price of such a locomotive engine, including the tender, is about £600 (4,200 Reichsthl.).

Each locomotive engine has an attendant who receives from the railway company one farthing per ton per mile (2¼ pfg.), that is, one half as much as the horse driver receives. For this payment he must provide the coal necessary for firing, as well as the lubricating oil, and also a helper, since two men are necessary to attend one locomotive engine. Assuming that such an engine brings daily to Stockton 1,000 cwt of coal, 20 miles, he will receive therefore a daily pay of 21 shillings (7 thl. 10 grs.). On the average, the monthly receipts of a locomotive engine attendant amount to £28 (196 thl.), out of which he must pay for the helper, the coal, the oil, etc.

Besides these two persons, however, two persons, who are paid day wages by the company, usually are required for attending to the 16–20 wagons.

From this statement it appears that the immediate expense of transport with locomotive engines is only half as much as with horses. If, however, the interest on capital expenditure is brought into account, as well as the very considerable cost of repairs to the locomotive engines, which at present does not admit of being arranged on a fixed basis, it will be seen that a large part of the saving is absorbed. It is maintained, also, and rightly so, that with transport by locomotive engines the wagons as well as the rails are more damaged than with horse traction. On these grounds it may be difficult to ascertain exactly how much advantage, or whether any advantage at all, results from traction by locomotive engines. At the time of our inspection, opinions were divided on this point, and exact figures were not yet available.[1]

Remarks about the Construction of Steam Locomotive Engines

And in particular

1. *Steam locomotive engines which are in use on the Darlington Railway*

The steam cylinders that supply the motive power stand perpendicular partly in the steam boiler and their upper ends project 12 in., exclusive of the flange. The boiler is cylindrical of plate ½ in. thick, 11½ ft long, and 4½ ft diameter, with a fire-tube 25 in. diameter, which lies 2 in. distant from the bottom; in front, this contains the grate, and at the opposite end finishes in the chimney, which projects about 8 ft above the boiler. Another boiler serving for a similar locomotive engine is cylindrical 10 ft 10 in. long, closed at one end by a hemisphere, and at the other end by a cast-iron plate. Its diameter is 4 ft 4 in.; the fire-tube, 26 in. diameter, does not lie in the centre but more towards one side and is joined by a semicircular formed end to a return tube 18½ in. diameter, which enters into the chimney at the end where the firing takes place. The boiler rests, by means of four short pipes or supports, which at their upper ends have flanges formed to the curvature of the boiler and below have horizontal flanges, resting upon a cast-iron frame that is 8 ft 2½ in. long, 3 ft 7 in. wide, and 8½ in. by $1\frac{1}{12}$ in. in section. Immediately under the supports lie the axles, either both in cast-iron tubes, or one in one such tube, and the other in plain bearings. The axles are round, 3½ to 3¾ in. diameter, and with a total length of 5 ft 2 in. After many trials, the wheels have been constructed in a lasting manner, as it is especially difficult to prepare large wheels for wagons on railways. These consist of two parts, an inner and an outer part, of cast-iron and fastened together with wooden wedges. The naves are round, internally bored accurately according to the diameter of the axles, and they are fastened by wedges in holes bored half in one and half in the other. The diameter of the inner part of the wheel is 30 in.; the outer part with the tread is 47 in. diameter. The depth of the nave is 5 in.; the width of the inner part of the wheel is 4 in.; this has twelve spokes $\frac{7}{12}$ to ¾ in. thick, which increase in width towards the middle. The spokes are bound together by a ring from 17 to 18¾ in. diameter. In the outer circumference, semicircular notches of $1\frac{5}{6}$ to

[1] *A consideration of how far this general description can be reconciled with other known records is given by J. G. H. Warren, op. cit., page* 116.—*Ed.*

2 in. diameter are arranged in the direction of each spoke so that exactly similar notches in the inner circumference of the outer part of the wheel coincide, and wooden wedges are driven in, so as to bind together the two parts. In new wheels the tread is $4\frac{1}{6}$ in. wide, and conical, diminishing towards the front $\frac{1}{6}$ in.; the thickness of metal in front is $1\frac{1}{4}$ in. and behind $1\frac{5}{6}$ in. The flange projects $\frac{3}{4}$ in. and the whole breadth of the wheel, inclusive of the flange, totals $5\frac{5}{6}$ in.; in some old wheels this is only $4\frac{1}{2}$ in. In the inner part a hole is arranged in which to set the crankpin, to which the connecting-rod of the cylinder is attached; the length of the crank arm is $11\frac{3}{4}$ in.; in another locomotive engine it is 10 in. Through the connecting-rods, one pair of wheels is connected with one cylinder and the other pair with the other cylinder. Because one cylinder must always stand at half-stroke in relation to the other, the wheels on one side of the engine are connected by horizontal coupling rods, and accordingly the crankpins are arranged so that two of the pins, in the diagonally opposite wheels, have special cranks fixed on them for the horizontal connecting-rods. The distance between the wheel centres is 5 ft 1 in. (in other cases 5 ft 3 in.). The connecting-rods are 8 ft long, and, in common with the whole arrangement of the straight line motion of the piston rods, are of wrought-iron. The connecting-rods are, with the latter, on a crossbar, which is itself attached to the end of a half-beam, the fulcrum of which is movable, and the straight line motion is obtained through the operation of counter-rods. These half-beams are double $33\frac{1}{4}$ in. long; the counter-rods are 15 in. long, and the lever for the turning of the fulcrum of the half-beam is $28\frac{1}{2}$ in. high. The fixed points for these different rods are arranged above on the boiler and stand out from the cylinder towards the middle.

The cylinders are regulated through perpendicular slide valves; the steam surrounds the valve. The pipe which leads the exhaust steam to the chimney into the atmosphere opens under the slide valve. The movement of the valve is 2 in. Attached to the middle of the horizontal coupling rods of the engine wheels are perpendicular rods, connected above with cranks standing at right angles on a shaft which revolves simultaneously with the engine wheels, and with the strokes of the cylinders. This shaft is the common valve shaft for both cylinders. On it are two excentrics, which are not fixed to it, but are movable round it, and are driven by hooks which engage in quadrant-shaped slots cut in them. By this means the pistons are caused to go backwards and forwards; the excentrics, or rather the hooks by which they are driven, stand on the shaft at right angles to one another. From each excentric leads the driving rod, which can be put in and out of gear with the levers which move the valves. This method of reversing the piston motion is the simplest and renders unnecessary many valve rods, which formerly were required in the application of the excentric. With this arrangement the change of motion can be undertaken with one cylinder, the other coming in to help, so as to bring the crankpins over the dead points.

On both sides of the boiler there is a platform 9 in. wide for the engine attendant; this lies just above the wheels. On one side there is a still higher plank by which all parts of the engine can be reached, and the valve gear adjusted.

The force pump which feeds the boiler with water is mounted on the side of the boiler and is moved by a rod which is attached to one of the half-beams. From this pump a leather hose leads to the water-cask, which is arranged on the wagon coupled next to the locomotive engine, and from which the boiler is fed.

The cylinders are high-pressure engines without condensation, the exhaust steam being discharged without further ado into the atmosphere.

It appears, therefore, that the construction of these steam locomotive engines is in general very simple.

There are two steam cylinders in order to achieve rotary motion without a flywheel by direct coupling of the engine wheels with the piston rods. The steam cylinders are of the simplest construction, and double-acting.

In practice, it is specially striking that many of the moving parts alter rapidly, a process accelerated by the continual shaking of the engine during motion. This is due mainly to the fact that it is scarcely possible to keep in one plane the four points of the rails on which the wheels of the engine rest. Therefore, the parts of the engine must yield somewhat, so that they may find their proper support.

2. *Steam locomotive engines which are planned for the Darlington Railway*

At the beginning of 1827, the engineers were occupied with the construction of some other locomotive engines. The designs prepared for these were communicated to us by Mr Hackworth[1] (mechanician in the service of the railway company). The most essential alteration is that the two cylinders are not to be one behind the other but side by side; that they are not to stand in the boiler, but on a cast-iron frame over or in front of the boiler; that the piston rods are not to work upwards but downwards. Both cylinders are to engage with the pair of wheels on one axle and the second pair of wheels is to be connected with the first by horizontal coupling rods. Thereby the construction will be simpler in many respects and the whole more secure.

In one project the engine has four wheels; the wheel centres are 5½ ft apart; the boiler is 9 ft long, and is 4½ ft in diameter; each cylinder is 10½ in. diameter and 22 in. stroke; the length of the connecting-rod is 3 ft 2 in.; the length of the half-beam, to the end of which the piston and connecting-rods are connected, is 3 ft; the lever for the fulcrum of the half-beam is 17 in. The valve gear shaft for both cylinders is suspended over the boiler, and is moved by the half-beam in the same manner as in the locomotive engine first described. The cylinder centres stand vertically over the crank pins in the wheels, and are 5½ ft apart.

The second project differs from the previous one only in that the engine has six wheels, so as to afford more supporting points to the boiler, and to increase the rolling friction of the engine, as its useful power subsists therein. In order that these wheels shall always bear on the rails, only the pair of wheels on which the connecting-rods work are mounted in fixed bearings; the other bearings are carried by balance beams so that the wheels can adjust themselves to the small unevennesses of the rails. The wheel centres are 4 ft 3 in. apart, the boiler is 12 ft 10 in. long, 4 ft 5 in. diameter, each cylinder is 10 in. diameter and 22 in. stroke. The engine wheels, inclusive of the flanges, are 50 in. in diameter.

In the third project the cylinders are in front of the boiler; the connecting-rods go out upwards. The cylinder centres stand 5½ ft apart; the cylinder diameter is 9 in. and the stroke 3 ft; but the connecting-rods are connected to the beam nearer to its fulcrum, and have therefore only 2 ft stroke; the whole length of the beam is 8 ft and the length of the connecting-rods is 6½ ft. The engine has six wheels, which are arranged as in the second project; the wheel centres are 4 ft 4 in. apart. The boiler is 13 ft long and is 4 ft 3 in. in diameter. The cylinders stand on the same plate on which the boiler rests, and on which are the bearings for the axles of the wheels. The latter are connected with one another by horizontal coupling rods. In this project may be seen something that has not been tested in practice with the usual construction of locomotive engines, namely, the position of the cylinders.

3. *Steam locomotive engine of Stephenson and Dickenson at Newcastle*

In the works of Stephenson and Dickenson[2] at Newcastle, a locomotive engine has been built

---

[1] *Timothy Hackworth* (1786–1850).—*Ed.*

[2] *This name appears in the German as 'Dickenson'. The name of the firm was at no time Stephenson and 'Dickenson' but Harris Dickinson occupied a prominent position in the works in* 1827 *as Financial Manager, an appointment necessitated by the absence of both George and Robert Stephenson on railway construction work elsewhere. Dickinson was probably a Quaker, and possibly nominated by Edward Pease* (1767–1858). *Simon Goodrich visited the works on* 26 *March* 1830 *and recorded in his journal that he saw 'Mr Dickinson who appeared as Manager or Partner'. The name of the partnership was Robert Stephenson & Co. from its formation on* 23 *June* 1823.—*Ed.*

recently (at the beginning of 1827) which so far has had no large-scale trial, but has been tested only in the workshop itself. In its construction and highly careful execution, it appears to surpass that hitherto employed. Also, regard is being paid to a better use of the fuel. Besides changes in the construction of the fire grate and boiler, there is this essential difference that the cylinders lie horizontally entirely in the boiler.

The boiler is of iron plate, with a strong cast-iron front plate; it is cylindrical 13 ft long and 4 ft diameter. In it lies, a few inches above the bottom, a firetube of 2 ft 3 in. diameter, wherein at the front end lies the firegrate, and which at the back communicates with a chimney of 20 in. diameter, and 16 ft high, and which can be raised 8 ft higher by means of a slide. On the under curvature of the chimney is a flap, which is fastened by cotters and can be removed easily in order to clean the chimney and the firetube. The grate consists of eight wrought-iron tubes, $1\frac{7}{8}$ in. inside diameter, $\frac{1}{4}$ in. thick, and 4 ft long. These open at the front end into a cast-iron box, on the front surface of which are eight openings which are closed with screws and serve for cleaning the grate bars. At the back end these grate bars open into a round tube of 20 in. diameter, which lies in the firetube; it is $3\frac{1}{2}$ (*sic*) ft long and reaches as far as underneath the chimney. This tube is in communication with the upper part of the boiler through a rectangular opening, which goes through the upper part of the flue space. The boiler itself is connected with the front iron box by two curved pieces of tube. The grate bars are constantly filled with water and form part of the boiler; also the firetube forms only a ring, which inside and outside is filled with water.

The cylinders lie over the firetube in the boiler, and are 9 in. diameter, and about $2\frac{1}{2}$ to 3 ft stroke. They are bolted by their flanges to the cast-iron front plate of the boiler. They are united with one another by a cast-iron piece through which steam is led to the slide valves, and the opening of which, close under the crown of the boiler, is provided with a valve movable from outside in order to regulate the entry of the steam. The exhaust steam flows from the cylinders through a sheet-iron tube lying in the boiler towards the chimney where both these tubes are bent upwards. Before the curved part, a descending tube leads out, which opens into a small waterbox lying under the chimney; this is used as a feed heater, from which the force pump, situated on the side of the boiler, lifts the feed water. In this way part of the exhaust steam is further used. The cylinder piston-rod is attached to the middle of a short arm, the ends of which are connected with the half-beams above and below. On the axis of the upper beam there is at the outer end a somewhat shorter lever arm which, through a connecting-rod, is united to the wheel of the engine. On the axle of the engine moved in this way are the excentrics which, through several coupling-rods, set in motion the slide valves lying, likewise, inside the boiler. The bearings of the upper half-beam are arranged on the front cast-iron plate, and on the cast-iron frame which carries the whole boiler. The wheels, and their connection by horizontal coupling-rods, are arranged in the same way as in the engines previously described.

This locomotive engine shares the improvements in those proposed for the Darlington Railway, with some not inconsiderable additions. The principal faults of the locomotives at present are that they are not constructed sufficiently durably, and therefore require many repairs. This locomotive engine works with 45 to 52 lb per sq. in. on the cylinder area, and should produce the effect of 15 horsepower.

General Remarks on Steam Locomotive Engines

As no opportunity will be afforded later in this report for treating the steam locomotive engine so completely, some historical notice will not be out of place here.

Messrs Trevithick and Vivian[1] in 1802 were the first to take out a patent for driving wagons by

[1] *The patent No.* 2599 *granted on* 24 *March* 1802 *to Richard Trevithick* (1771–1833) *and his cousin, Andrew Vivian.—Ed.*

steam engines according to the expansion principle; in 1804 they tried such a locomotive engine on the Merthyr Tydwill (*sic*) Railway in South Wales. This engine drew the freight wagons by means of the friction of the wheels on the railway, and therefore could not be used where the railway was steeply graded. In the patent they described the engine as having a horizontal steam cylinder with a flywheel, and an axle moved by a crank and coupled with the wheel-axles by toothed wheels. Mr Blenkinsop[1] in 1811 took out a patent for the use of a toothed rail for drawing the wagons. Such a locomotive engine was erected on the railway from Middleton Colliery to Leeds, and is still (1827) working thereon. This kind of locomotive engine has been copied many times, among other places at the Horlot Colliery near Liége, but without success; so also with the attempts that were made to place them in operation at Saarbrücken and in Silesia. Mr Blackett[2] in 1813 set in motion a locomotive engine on Trevithick's principle, on the railway at the Wylam Colliery near Newcastle, which drew forward the wagons only by the friction of the wheels on the rails. Messrs W. and T. Chapmann[3] in 1812 held a patent for a locomotive engine which was moved by a toothed wheel engaging with a stretched-out chain laid along the middle of the line; this method was tried on the Hetton Railway[4] near Newcastle, but without success.

Mr Brunton,[5] of Butterley Ironworks, took out a patent in 1813 for a very ingenious method of driving locomotive engines. The piston-rods set forks in motion, which moved like legs, and, since they could not slip upon the ground, the engine was propelled at each stroke. Meanwhile Mr Blackett continued with zeal his experiments with locomotive engines which worked only by the rolling friction, and proved that this was sufficient to perform a useful effect when the railway is level or has a very slight gradient. Nevertheless, the early Trevithick locomotive engines built were very imperfect. At the beginning of 1814, G. Stephenson built a locomotive engine at Killingworth Colliery, with two cylinders, each 8 in. diameter by 2 ft stroke, a cylindrical boiler 8 ft long and 34 in. diameter, and with a firetube 20 in. diameter through it. The connecting-rods, which were in direct connection with the cylinder piston-rods, moved two toothed wheels of 12 in. diameter, which through one equally large wheel were maintained in their correct positions; these drove two toothed wheels of 24 in. diameter, which were fixed on the axles of the engine wheels. This locomotive engine drew eight coal wagons, together weighing 600 cwt on a $\frac{1}{456}$ ascending railway at a speed of 5·6 ft per second. This engine worked regularly for some time, until a continual jolting arose through the connection of the toothed wheels, which increased as the wheel teeth became worn. This caused Mr Stephenson, in conjunction with Mr Dood (*sic*), to take out a patent[6] in 1815 for a locomotive engine in which the movement of the piston rods was communicated to the wheels in a more practicable manner. The crankpins for the connecting-rods were fixed directly in the engine wheels, which were so connected with the cylinder piston-rods. The crankpins must always stand at right angles to one another, therefore the wheels are coupled together by horizontal rods, or by

[1] *John Blenkinsop* (1783–1831). *Patent No.* 3431 *of* 10 *April* 1811. *The first locomotive, built by Matthew Murray* (1765–1826), *was tried on* 24 *June* 1812. *When the second engine was ready, a regular locomotive service across Hunslet Moor was inaugurated on* 12 *August* 1812. *This was the first commercial use of steam locomotives with flanged wheels, and the line was also the first rack railway.—Ed.*

[2] *Christopher Blackett, the owner of Wylam Colliery.—Ed.*

[3] *The names are thus given in the German text. The patent is doubtless No.* 3632 *of* 30 *December* 1812 *granted to William Chapman* (1749–1832) *and his brother, Edward Walton Chapman.—Ed.*

[4] *The German text gives Hetton, probably copying page* 131 *of the first edition* (1825) *of Nicholas Wood's 'Practical Treatise on Rail-Roads'. It was, however, corrected to Heaton in the errata and in the later editions. The trial was made at Heaton Colliery, near Newcastle upon Tyne.—Ed.*

[5] *William Brunton, who was engaged in* 1796 *by Boulton and Watt as a mechanic, left the firm in* 1808 *to join the Butterley Ironworks. His locomotive patent was No.* 3700 *of* 22 *May* 1813. *In* 1821 *Brunton became managing partner in the Eagle Foundry, Birmingham, where he produced the first mechanical stoker.—Ed.*

[6] *Patent No.* 3887 *of* 28 *February* 1815 *granted to George Stephenson* (1781–1848) *and Ralph Dodds* (1792–1874). *Dodds at that time was viewer at Killingworth Colliery.—Ed.*

an endless chain stretched over two special wheels fixed to the middle of the axles, and so are always maintained in the same position in relation to one another. This endless chain is still used on several locomotive engines in the neighbourhood of Newcastle and Sunderland. Later, Stephenson together with Mr Losh made an improvement[1] in steam locomotive engines, but this we have not seen in use. The tubes on which the boiler stands were provided inside with quite thick pistons, and were open above so that the steam, through the water in the boiler, might press on the pistons and transmit this pressure to the axle bearings. This arrangement was employed especially on six-wheeled locomotive engines and by it the load was uniformly distributed over all the wheels.

This arrangement was employed for some time on the locomotives on the Killingworth Colliery Railway, but by May 1827 it had been discarded, and the axle bearings were firmly connected with the frame and boiler. The valve gear used at present is the same as that previously described. Formerly, a rectangular frame which was pushed forwards and backwards by the excentric was employed. However, this did not open and close the valves at the same time for both directions of motion of the engine, and on this account introduced irregularities in its working; therefore this method was discarded, although it is still found on some engines. The parallel motion of the cylinder piston rods is so arranged that the crossbars to which they as well as the connecting-rods are attached, move up and down in a vertical line.

The locomotive engine at the Wylam Colliery, near Newcastle, runs upon a (German) railway of cast-iron; its wheels are without flanges. It has eight such wheels and a wooden frame, on which the cylinders stand upright beside the boiler. The engine wheels are coupled by a train of toothed wheels set in motion by a toothed wheel on the axle of which the cranks are fixed. It is probably the only locomotive engine which runs on this type of railway. The eight wheels distribute the weight of the engine over more points of the railway, which otherwise would have been too weak to support it.

(c) Transport on the inclined planes

At Greenfield on the high ground between two inclined planes are two steam-engines of Watt type working together, with cylinder diameters of 21 in. Engl., which together are adequate to develop 30 horsepower. At Brusselton there are two similar engines, but each of 30 in. cylinder diameter, and together giving 60 horsepower.

Both the Brusselton and the Greenfield engines draw up at one time eight loaded wagons holding respectively one chaldron of coal; as soon as these have reached the top, they are lowered together by means of a brake arrangement. The descending wagons could have been used as a counterbalance for those which are to be drawn up; this, however, is not done, as the steam-engines have adequate power and the waiting of one load for another causes delay. The steam-engines would be able to draw up twelve loaded wagons at one time without difficulty.

The whole load to be raised or lowered amounts to:—

8 empty wagons	160 cwt (Centner)
8 chaldrons of coal at 53 cwt ..	424 ,, ,,
Total	584 ,, ,,

This load is made fast to a rope of 7¼ in. circumference (2⅓ in. Engl. diameter), which is wound on a cylindrical drum.[2]

[1] *Patent No.* 4067 *of* 30 *September* 1816 *granted to William Losh* (1770–1861) *and George Stephenson.—Ed.*

[2] The best ropes were made by John Grimshaw of Bishop Wearmouth, not far from Sunderland, on a machine specially contrived for the purpose, which though 10 ft high, occupied only 24 sq. ft of floor space. It is said that they are able to make, on this machine, 13 in. cables of 100 fathoms (600 ft) long, and 3½ in. ropes for inclined planes of 1,500 fathoms (9,000 ft) long, in one piece. In the same factory, also, a flat rope of exceptional quality was made by a new method. (*Footnote by Authors.*)

The Brusselton engine has a 5 ft stroke and makes about 20 revolutions a minute, which gives $20 \times 1{\cdot}822 = 36{\cdot}44$ revolutions of the rope drum. The rope drum can be reckoned to have a mean diameter of 5½ ft Engl., and hence winds 207·6 yards of rope a minute. The longest inclined plane of 1,851 yards is therefore surmounted in 8 minutes 57 seconds. Nevertheless, the engine can run considerably faster and this length can be travelled in 6 minutes.

The steam-engine was intended originally for a steamboat; the beams lie below and the coupling-rods are connected with the piston-rods by a crosshead. Each cylinder is 90½ in. high and stands on an iron tank. The air pump piston-rod is hung from an ordinary crosshead like that of the cylinder piston; the connecting rods of the latter are, however, prolonged as far as the first (10½ ft long), and are here tied together with a pair of arms 2 ft 10½ in. long. Attached to the ends of the connecting-rods for the air pumps are radius rods of 2 ft 5⅛ in. long, whereby the movement of the piston rod is made approximately rectilinear. Each engine has two beams, and each of them consists of two cast-iron plates 3¼ in. apart. From centre to centre they are 11 ft 9 in. long, in the middle 1 ft 11½ in. high; at the attachment points of the rods at the ends 3½ in.; the rim is 1¼ in. thick and the filling ¾ in. thick. The connecting-rod is 8 ft long between centres, and the cranks of both engines are attached at right angles on a shaft 11 ft 2 in. long. In the middle of this shaft there is a large toothed wheel with 224 wooden teeth 9¾ in. wide and 16¼ in. diameter. This engages with a smaller toothed wheel entirely of iron, with 88 teeth and of 6 ft 5 in. diameter. On the same shaft there is a bevel wheel of 63 teeth and 4 ft diameter, to which is fixed a disengaging coupling; the latter engages with a second bevel wheel of 88 teeth and 5½ in. diameter, the axis of which lies at right angles to the rails. Upon this shaft is the rope drum of 4 ft diameter and 6 ft long; the centre of it lies 11 ft above the rails. On one side of the rope drum is a rim 8 ft in diameter and on the other side a brake wheel of the same diameter covered on the outside with wood. The brake consists of a strong wrought-iron band completely encircling the wheel; the band can be tightened by compound levers. The two boilers are cylindrical 15⅝ ft long, 7½ ft in diameter, with flues which run round the sides.

The Greenfield engine does not run so quickly. It has only a 3 ft stroke, and makes over 40 revolutions a minute, which corresponds to about 20 revolutions of the drum.

This engine is generally of the same construction, and arrangement of its parts, as the engine at Brusselton; it also has two cylinders, etc.

The beams of this engine are worthy of notice; they are 8 ft 8 in. long and each consists of two wrought-iron plates $\frac{9}{16}$ in. thick, which stand 2⅜ in. apart and are united by screws. In the middle and chiefly where shafts go through it, pieces of cast iron are placed between the plates. On each side of the cylinder lies one such beam, which therefore is secured completely against side bending. It will not be easy to get beams which possess greater power of resistance for so small a weight. On many occasions it would be very useful to secure cheap and easily constructed beams which are less subject to breakage than is cast-iron.

In the mechanical workshops of Messrs Stephenson and Dickenson[1] in Newcastle, the following prices were given to us for steam-engines built in the factory. The pound sterling may be reckoned as the equivalent[2] of 7 Reichsthaler in Berlin.

Steam locomotive engines of 8 horsepower .. 3,850 Reichsthaler (*£550*)

Stationary or fixed steam-engines. High-pressure Watt type of

8 horsepower	..	2,100 to 2,450 Reichsthaler	(*£300 to £350*)
12 „	..	3,150 to 3,500 „	(*£450 to £500*)
16 „	..	4,505 to 5,040 „	(*£650 to £720*)

[1] *See footnote[2] at page 18.—Ed.*

[2] *The German text gives prices only in Reichsthaler. The English sterling equivalents shown in italics have been converted on the basis given by the Authors.—Ed.*

20	„	.. 5,600 to 6,300	„	(*£800 to £900*)
30	„	.. 8,400 to 9,450	„	(*£1,200 to £1,350*)

A set of improved wagon wheels, boxes, axles, etc., 1,050 Reichsthaler (*£15*) free on board ship at Newcastle. These prices vary in proportion to the wages, etc., and hold good as average terms, payment through London, by bills of exchange, 3 months after despatch. Address:—

Robert Stephenson & Comp.
Engineers and founders in Newcastle upon Tyne

After the foregoing general remarks, we now pass on to the detailed description of the several parts of the railway and the stationary machinery connected with it.

Rails of Rolled Wrought-Iron

The rails (*malleable iron rails*), of which this railway is constructed, are of wrought-iron, rolled out between rollers at a single heat, and the bar must pass between the rolls six times before the rail is finished. Most of them are made at the Bedlington Iron Works, near Morpeth, 8 miles from Newcastle.

Such a rail, Fig. 1, has its upper face 2 in. wide, with the edges rounded so that the greatest width is 2¼ in. Beneath this is a strengthening rib which, where the rail rests on the cast-iron supports, is 1½ in. high and ½ in. thick at the lower edge. Between these supporting points, which lie 3 ft apart, a swelling is formed which increases up to 1 in. higher, so that the total height of the rail is 3¼ in., and the thickness at the lower edge is ¾ in.

Each rail is 5 yards (15 ft Engl.) long, and weighs 28 lb a yard. A ton (20 cwt of 112 lb) of these rails costs £13 10*s.* (94 thl. 15 grs.). In the summer of 1828 the price has been reduced to £12 (84 thl.), free in Newcastle. Therefore 1 yard of this rail costs 3*s.* 5*d.* to 3*s.* (1 thl. 4 grs. 2 pfg. to 1 thl. 1 grs. 6 pfg.), or an English foot run of railway with two rails costs 2*s.* 3⅓*d.* to 2*s.* (22 grs. 9⅓ pfg. to 21 grs.). A cast-ron rail of equal capacity would have to weigh 56 lb a yard, and, since a ton of cast-iron rails costs just as much, or almost as much, as a ton of wrought-iron rails, so might cast-iron rails be rated twice as costly as wrought-iron.

Herein lies an essential superiority of the wrought-iron rails. This price relation in England, which is so favourable for wrought-iron rails, now appears to be the opposite to that which applies in Germany. One of the Moselle ironworks (Grossh. Niederrhein)[1], which delivers bar-iron at 42 thl. per 1,000 lb, will deliver these wrought-iron rails at 63 thl. per 1,000 lb, when half a million pounds are ordered, or 57 thl. when one million pounds are ordered. Cast rails stand at 25 thl. per 1,000 lb; and therefore are still cheaper than wrought-iron, even although they must be made more than twice as heavy in order to give them equal strength. Such rails cost for a Prussian cwt:—

In England	In Rhenish Prussia
4 thl. 24 grs.– 4 thl. 7 grs.	6 thl. 28 grs.– 6 thl. 8 grs.
or per 1,000 lb	
43 thl. 20 grs.–38 thl. 24 grs.	63 thl. –57 thl.

A fathom run of railway (comprising 2 fathoms of rail) of this kind weighs 123¾ lb and costs:—

5 thl. 10 grs. 6 pfg.–4 thl. 21 grs. 7 pfg.	7 thl. 21 grs. 9 pfg.–6 thl. 29 grs. 5 pfg.

A Prussian mile of 2,400 ft of such railway weighs 4,014⅓ cwt and costs:—

19,268 thl. 25 grs.–16,994 thl.	27,832 thl. 22 grs.–25,156 thl. 16 grs.

According to this, these rails cost from 44 to 48 per cent more than in England.

[1] *The Grand Duchy of the Lower Rhine, a Prussian territory.—Ed.*

Other intrinsic advantages are:—

(1) That they are much less subject to the risk of breakage than are cast-iron rails.

(2) That they readily permit a little bending, and that therefore the curves of the railway can be formed more regularly than is possible with cast-iron rails.

(3) These rails are 15 ft long, whereas cast-iron rails are not easily made more than 4 ft long, so that there are fewer rail joints in the proportion of 4 to 15 (or nearly one-fourth), a very substantial advantage whereby the motion of the loaded wagons is facilitated and made uniform, more than one at first sight would believe.

(4) Finally, these wrought-iron rails can be fastened more securely than is possible with cast-iron rails; also the friction on them is less than on the latter.

Cast-iron Chairs for the Rails

The wrought-iron rails are fastened in cast-iron chairs, some of which rest on wooden and others on stone sleepers; the latter are now preferred and are replacing wooden sleepers little by little. The stone sleepers are made from a somewhat coarse-grained sandstone of ordinary quality, and are squared only roughly. We found one such sleeper 21 in. long, 10 in. high, and 14 in. wide; but the dimensions are very variable. The early cast chairs had a projecting rim on the under face round the fastening holes (Fig. *2a*); this was from $2\frac{1}{8}$ in. to $2\frac{1}{2}$ in. diameter, and projected $\frac{1}{2}$ in. On the stone, a seat for the chair and these projections was chiselled out, and two holes bored 4 in. deep; the chair was then fixed on the stone by two wooden plugs. It was found, however, that water collected in the chiselled-out seats so that the wooden plugs soon became rotten; the current practice, therefore, is to omit the rims round the holes (Fig. *3a*), and merely to chisel flat the face of the stone where the chair is to rest. The transverse wooden sleepers formerly used extended across under the railway, but these at present are being replaced by stone sleepers which are provided only in blocks. The rails are fastened in the chairs by small transverse pins which pass through the chairs, of which the corresponding holes are shown in the drawing (Fig. 1). Those chairs in which two rails butt together are made in the same manner as those which support the rail in the middle.

Fastening the Rails in the Chairs by Wedges

It has been found that the pins just mentioned easily become damaged, so that, when they once become loose, they cannot again be made tight; it is now intended to introduce a wedge fastening (Fig. *3a, b*). These chairs have a rounded notch, as shown in Fig. *3a*, wherein fits the wedge; this is made of wrought-iron, or better still, of steel which can penetrate somewhat into the rail. The wedge is shaped to this notch on one side, while the other side is flat so as to lie close against the rail. Those chairs which are to receive the ends of two rails have the same dimensions as the others which merely support the rail at the intermediate points, but, in addition to the notches for the wedges, they have two small holes in the side walls, just as in the older chairs, so that the rail ends may be fastened therein by pins. Two wedges are used also in these joint chairs, and they are inserted in opposite directions. The fastening of the rails in the chairs, and especially at their ends, is a not unimportant object. By means of the wedges, the advantage is secured with little trouble of being able to tighten the rails afresh firmly. The holes in the baseplate of the chair, Fig. *3b*, which serve to fasten to the stone deeper, are cast somewhat conical. The older chairs are 6 in. long at the base, $3\frac{1}{4}$ in. wide, and 1 in. thick; the small side walls are $1\frac{1}{2}$ in. high; and the holes for driving in the wooden plugs are $1\frac{1}{3}$ in. diameter. In the newer chairs, the baseplate is 6 in. long, $4\frac{1}{2}$ in. wide, and $\frac{3}{4}$ in. thick. The side walls are only $3\frac{3}{8}$ in. wide, and the thickness of the chair, where the rail bears on it, is $1\frac{1}{8}$ in. The holes for the wooden plugs are $1\frac{1}{8}$ in. diameter at the top, and $\frac{11}{12}$ in. at the bottom; the holes for the transverse pins are $\frac{3}{8}$ in. diameter.

Where the railway passes over high-roads, it is necessary to place the sleepers on which the chairs are fixed so deep under the surface that an adequate stone covering can lie thereon. For this purpose the chair shown in Fig. 4*a*, *b* is used; it differs from the ordinary one in its greater height. The baseplate of this chair is 8 in. long, $3\frac{1}{2}$ in. wide, and 1 in. thick; the height to the resting point of the rail is 5 in.

Cast-iron Rails

In addition to the wrought-iron rails, cast-iron rails were at first employed, but these are being exchanged gradually for wrought-iron rails. These cast-iron rails are cast at Newcastle in accordance with the Patent of Losh and Bell[1] and are generally similar to those which are employed on the Hetton Railway. These rails are cut at each end (but on opposite sides) back to the centre line for a short distance, so forming opposing laps which fit into one another and thus rest together in the chairs. The rail and one lap (that is the running length of the rail) is 4 ft Engl. or $46\frac{1}{2}$ in. Pruss. long; each lap is $2\frac{1}{2}$ in. long and $3\frac{1}{4}$ in. high; in the middle the total height of the rail is 6 in.; the width at the top is $2\frac{1}{3}$ in.; the height of this part is $1\frac{2}{3}$ in., which is reduced at the sides to $\frac{1}{2}$ in. This is the thickness of the web part, which in the middle is $3\frac{1}{3}$ in. high, and ends below in a strengthening rib which is 1 in. high and $1\frac{1}{4}$ in. wide and has sharp corners below. One such rail weighs 65 lb, and 1 yard would weigh $48\frac{3}{4}$ lb. These rails, therefore, are not quite double as heavy as the wrought-iron rails, which weigh 28 lb a yard. The chairs upon which these rails rest are 8 in. long, $3\frac{1}{2}$ in. wide, and 4 in. high. The rail seat is arc-shaped and has a chord of 3 in., and a rise of $\frac{5}{6}$ in.; it will be described in greater detail in connection with the Hetton Railway.

Sidings or Passing Places

The connections with the sidings are made of cast-iron by reason of its greater firmness and simpler construction, as parts can be made in one piece in this material which otherwise could be made only of separate parts fastened together. At every siding, Fig. 9, three different cast-iron pieces are required, namely: first, where the two rails cross one another, Fig. 5*a*, *b*, *c*; second, where the inner rail of the siding joins the main line, Fig. 6*a*, *b*, *c*; and third, where the outer rail of the siding joins the main line, Fig. 8. These pieces consist of a cast-iron plate, which is provided on the upper surface with the necessary rail pieces on which the wagons can run; with the chairs required for attaching the abutting wrought-iron rails; and underneath with the requisite strengthening ribs and with holes in the plate for fixing it to the stone sleepers. The first piece, Fig. 5*a*, is 4 ft long, 1 ft wide at the ends, and 6 in. wide in the middle; at the side where thc two lines run together a groove is provided $1\frac{1}{4}$ in. wide and 1 in. deep, the side walls of which form the continuation of the rails, and which admits the wheel flange on whichever side it may run. At the end where the lines diverge, the groove is divided into two parts, each of which widens up to $2\frac{1}{2}$ in. The sharp wedge in between joins on to the rails, to accommodate which two chairs are cast on each end; the rails are fixed in the chairs with pins. On the under side are two strengthening ribs, $\frac{1}{2}$ in. thick and $2\frac{1}{2}$ in. high in the middle. These pieces are fixed on two stones by means of four plugs. The two other pieces, Fig. 6*a*, *b*, *c* and Fig. 8, consists of a similar cast-iron plate; on which a ledge serves as a rail, and chairs are provided to connect the wrought-iron rails, one chair at one end and two at the other. In the continuation of the second rail, which adjoins the first on one side, is a forged iron movable tongue,

[1] *Presumably, this refers to William Losh and Thomas Bell, his partner. The patent is probably No.* 4067 *of* 30 *September* 1816, *granted to William Losh and George Stephenson, previously mentioned.—Ed.*

Fig. 7, that tapers to a point. This tongue is 3 ft long, 2¼ in. wide, and 1¼ in. high. It is movable about a pin fixed in the plate, so that the wagons will take to the main line or to the siding according as the tongue lies against the rail or away from it. So that the tongue shall not be moved by the side pressure of the wheel flange, a small iron plate ½ in. thick and 5 in. long, cut somewhat wedge-shaped, 3¼ in. to 2¼ in. wide, and fastened to a small chain (see Fig. 9) is placed between the tongue and a projection on the plate, and in this way the tongue is kept pressed against the rail. In order to hold the tongue away from the rail, there is a notch in the plate in which a thin plate can be placed. This, however, is not used, as the guidance of the wagons would not be affected even if the tongue were pushed accidentally too near the rail, as the wheel flange would push it back again easily. The movable tongue should always be set so that the wagons keep to the main line, and ought to be moved only when a wagon train needs to take to the siding; immediately afterwards it should be restored to the former position. Excluding the portions which serve as chairs for the wrought-iron rails, these pieces are 4 ft long, and the plates are about 5 in. wide, and 1 in. thick; on the underside are two strengthening ribs, one of which is immediately under the side serving as a rail; these ribs are ½ in. thick and up to 2½ in. high in the middle.

Instead of these pieces with the movable tongues, especially at first, separate chairs were used for the wrought-iron rails, and to these a plate was attached to which was fixed the pin on which the tongue turned, Fig. 10*a*, *b*, *c*. The underplate is 5¼ in. wide, 7¼ in. long, and 1 in. thick; the chair is formed in the usual way; for the reception of the pin there is a tubular projection, 3 in. long, on the underside. The complete arrangement, Fig. 12, is simpler than the cast-iron pieces, but affords less security; in front, the point of the tongue rests only on a cast-iron chair which is provided with a projection to prevent it from slipping off. As such heavy cast-iron pieces are not required and the wrought-iron rails suffice, so this arrangement is cheaper than that previously described. At the sidings, however, it is important that the wagons should be directed safely, and not be endangered by running off the rails. For that reason, three check rails are employed at each siding, Fig. 9, namely: where one line crosses the other; on the inner sides of both outer rails, that of the main line and that of the siding; and where one line joins the other, on the inner side of that rail of the main line from which branches the outer rail of the siding. The wheel flange is on the inner side of the rail, and when the wheels on one side of the wagon encounter this check rail it is impossible for the wagons to come out of the line into which they should be guided, either by an oblique pull or in any other manner. These check rails are usually wrought-iron rails, which lie 1 in. from the other; they are 7 ft long and at both ends they are bent away from the running rail, so that they form a sort of mouth which the wheel flange cannot miss. The check rail lies $\frac{7}{12}$ to 1⅓ in. higher than the other rail, and rests with it upon suitably shaped chairs, Fig. 12*a*, *b*, which at the bottom are 9¾ in. long and 3½ in. wide; the chairs are fixed to the stone sleepers by two plugs.

The whole length of a siding is from 340 to 400 ft, and it is separated from the main line by a space of between 4 and 5 ft, or about the width of the railway. From the point of intersection of the two inner rails up to the junction point of the siding with the main line is 41 ft, and the rails therefore make an angle of 6°.16′.47″ with one another. The total length of the steam locomotive engine, the tender, and 20 one-chaldron wagons coupled to one another, amounts to not more than 180 ft, so that the siding is in a position to take two such trains at the same time, and to allow another train to pass on the main line.

Guiding Rollers for the Inclined Planes

On the inclined planes, cast-iron guiding rollers, or sheaves, over which the rope runs, are arranged in the middle of the track and 24 ft apart.

These cast-iron rollers are keyed fast on a wrought-iron axle 9¾ in. long and ⅝ in. diameter, which lies in wooden bearings $1\frac{7}{8}$ in. long that are fastened to cast-iron supports. The supports for these rollers consist of a single piece of cast-iron in which are fixed the wooden linings which serve as bearings for the axles. These supports are fixed to a wooden sleeper by four screwbolts; the baseplate is $9\frac{3}{4}$ in. square and 1 in. thick, and the height 8 in. The wood linings are reduced at both ends, so that they are secure without further fastening. The sheaves have an outside diameter of $12\frac{1}{2}$ in., and a groove $2\frac{1}{2}$ in. deep for the reception of the rope; they are $4\frac{3}{4}$ in. wide, and are light iron castings; the thickness of the side-walls of the groove is only $\frac{1}{4}$ in.

Wheels for Railway Wagons

For the wagons that travel on the railway, several kinds of cast-iron wheels have been employed, which are all fixed on forged iron axles, so that the latter must rotate in bearings. All these wheels have chilled (case-hardened) rims, as experience had shown that these hardened rims not only rolled with little friction but also lasted considerably longer. The chief difficulty with such wheels lies in the unequal contraction of the cast-iron in cooling, because the circumference of the wheel is quickly and suddenly chilled in casting, while the iron in the middle is still fluid, and so the centre of the wheel as it cools draws the circumference strongly towards it. Therefore, the spokes tend either to crack or are, at least, in such a state of tension that they are not able to offer much resistance, and will break under a moderate shock. Many experiments have been made to remedy this drawback, and Fig. 13*a*, *b* represents a wheel in which this object is best achieved. In these wheels the spokes and rim are cast in one piece, and this constitutes the chief advantage. To obviate the unequal contraction, the mould of the nave of the wheel is cut through and in the slot a thin iron plate is fixed, whereby the spokes become free to yield, and the parts are duly drawn together. These slots, which, in the mould, are scarcely a line ($\frac{1}{12}$ in.) wide, expand in the cooling, often to more than $\frac{1}{4}$ in. The wheel has twelve spokes, which are slightly sinuous, a shape which allows the parts to draw together better. When this wheel is to be fitted on the axle, the slots are tightly filled with two wrought iron wedge pieces, and, on both sides of the nave, wrought-iron bands are fitted 1 in. thick and $1\frac{1}{8}$ in. wide. These bands are put on hot and contract tightly on the nave on cooling. When, in this manner the nave is firmly united, its inside forms a square box, $3\frac{1}{2}$ in. wide at the back and a little reduced towards the front to 3 in., on a length of $5\frac{1}{4}$ in.

The axle, which at this part is likewise square, is placed in this box and is fastened by wooden wedges, into which, better still, iron wedges are driven.

A linchpin is therefore superfluous; except to serve the particular purpose of preventing the wheel from sliding forward so as to become loose on the axle, which would directly produce a great disadvantage in the motion of the wheel.

Two other forms of wheel construction are often used, but these agree with the first described, except in the spokes. With both of these kinds, the spokes are of wrought-iron and are joined to the rim and nave by the casting, whereby it was hoped to avoid unequal contraction. With one kind there are 10 round spokes 1 in. diameter. It soon appears in practice that these wheels were not sufficiently durable, in that the spokes rapidly became loose. Another form of construction was, therefore, adopted. Here the spokes are $\frac{1}{2}$ in. thick and 2 in. wide, and are likewise cast in the nave. To make this connection more secure, two small holes, about $\frac{1}{2}$ in. diameter, are drilled through the spokes at both ends; and through these the cast-iron flows so that the spokes should be secured more firmly in the nave and rim. But these spokes, also, became loose in use and rendered the wheels unserviceable. In front, the nave is usually provided with a wrought-iron band, which, however, is not necessary here, although it was so with the first described wheels. In these wheels the sinuate shape of the spokes is purposeless.

Generally, these wheels are about 30 in. in diameter and the rim is from 3 to $3\frac{1}{4}$ in. wide; in addition, the flange projects from $\frac{3}{4}$ to 1 in. in a sloping direction. The outside of the rim is slightly conical; this varies in different wheels from $\frac{1}{8}$ to $\frac{1}{4}$ in., and serves partly to reduce the rubbing of the flange on the rails, and partly also to ease the motion of the wagon round curves; as the wagon has a tendency to continue moving in a straight direction, the wheel flange will lie against the rail on the convex (*sic*) part of the line, so that the wheel runs on a layer diameter than the opposite one which runs on the shorter concave (*sic*) line of the railway, and so the wagon will accommodate itself to the curve.

The thickness of the rim at the front is from $\frac{1}{2}$ to $\frac{5}{8}$ in., but increases near the flange to $1\frac{1}{8}$ in. and $1\frac{1}{2}$ in. In the wheels with wrought-iron spokes, the rim has a strengthening rib $\frac{1}{2}$ in. high on the inside; there is also a collar fixed on the inner side of the nave which projects $1\frac{3}{4}$ in. beyond the outside diameter (7 in.) of the nave. This collar has been omitted as superfluous in the newer wheels.

In addition to the three kinds of wheels described, of which the first is by far the best, others have been tried, but the variations were immaterial.

The weight of these 30 in. wheels ranges from 252 lb to 280 lb, and those illustrated in Fig. 13 with cast-iron spokes are the heavier.

The durability of these wheels is very variable. Many wheels with wrought-iron spokes were useless after only 14 days; others lasted over three months and even a year; a durability of 14 months was the maximum. The life attained was not governed by the wheel rim itself having worn out, but because the spokes had failed. These wheels with cast-iron spokes have been in use only a short time, but promise so well that already their superiority may be considered as decided. We saw very many wheels with broken rims, and this may be considered as proof that the wheel rims are cast too weak for the heavy loads, the severe shocks, and the velocity of the motion, particularly on the inclined planes.

The arrangement for case-hardening the castings of these wheels is shown in the drawing (Fig. 14*a*, *b*, *c*, *d*). Fig. 14*a*, *b* shows a cast-iron case $1\frac{3}{4}$ in. thick at the bottom, $4\frac{1}{4}$ in. high, and 30 in. inside diameter. The inner face is turned closely to the outside diameter of the wheel, and is coated with fish-oil, or with a mixture of fish-oil and graphite, so that the fluid iron shall not cling to it. The cast-iron case is surrounded by two wrought-iron bands, because it might crack through the repeated heatings. The case is laid flat on the floor of the foundry, and the wheel formed with moulding sand while the wooden pattern, which fits closely inside the case, is lying therein. The pattern is then withdrawn, so that the cast-iron case forms the wall, against which the rim of the wheel must cool down. Upon this, the upper part of the mould-box is fixed, which usually consists of an iron box Fig. 14*c*, *d*. This forms a low cylinder with six or eight spokes and a polygon in the centre and between which are interlaced wires to support the moulding sand. Two openings serve for pouring in the iron. Four pegs enable the cover to be lifted or lowered by means of a crane. Two tenons correspond with two places on the case where two guiding pieces are screwed on; between these the tenons pass, so that the cover may lie accurately on the case, as shown by Fig. 14*d*. The metal is poured in simultaneously through both cover holes; it is grey soft pig-iron, which is melted down in the cupola and is drawn off in pans; it is not good to pour the metal too hot. A case-hardened wheel shows in the fracture, on the outer side of the rim, a white ring of a peculiar radiant texture, which often penetrates to a depth of $\frac{1}{2}$ in., while the inner part of the wheel is of ordinary pig-iron. The outer surface of the rim is so smooth, that it does not need further turning.[1]

---

[1] Similar wheels have been introduced on the Bohemian Railway from Budweis to Mauthhausen, which were cast by Mariazell and Blansko.

These are, in front, $30\frac{1}{8}$ in., and at the flange $30\frac{3}{8}$ in. diameter, and are 3 in. wide; the flange stands $1\frac{1}{4}$ in. above the rim; they have 12 spokes $\frac{1}{2}$ in. thick, a nave 5 in. outside diameter and $5\frac{1}{2}$ in. long; the nave is cast with slots in three or four places; originally they were cast with a round hole for the axle, but lately they have been cast whole and then bored out after the wedging and the fixing of two wrought-iron bands, which are $\frac{5}{8}$ in.

Axles and Axle-bearings for the Wagons

As previously stated, the wheels are fixed to the axles by wooden wedges, the two wheels on one axle. The axles (Fig. 15) are of wrought-iron 2⅝ in. diameter where they run in the bearings; the ends, which are fixed in the wheels, are square and tapered towards the front. The weight of such an axle is from 98 to 126 lb, and yet it appears already that these axles have bent under the load. A pound of wrought-iron is worth 3*d.* (2½ grs.);[1] therefore, such an axle costs £1 4*s.* 6*d.* to £1 11*s.* 6d.; or 6 thl. 17 grs. 3 pfg. to 10 thl. 10 grs. 9 pfg. The turned part which lies in the bearing is 11 ⅞in. long; the part keyed in the wheel nave is 7½ in. long, 2½ in. square in front, and 3 in. square at the back. The axle is provided at the ends with holes for the linchpins; the middle part is octagonal 2¾ in. thick and 25⅝ in. long, so that, therefore, the inner sides of the wheels must stand at least 49⅜ in. from one another. This should give a free play of about ⅝ in. between the rail and the wheel flange, but by reason of the rounding of the wheel flange this cannot be determined closely.

The bearings at present used most frequently on these wagons, see Fig. 16*a*, *b* and Fig. 17, are very simple, but not entirely satisfactory, as they are not able to retain the lubricant, which drips off soon after it is applied. For this reason, many other arrangements have been tried, one of which seems likely to be effective. The first consists only of a half-bearing of cast-iron, Fig. 16*a*, *b*, which is situated above the axle, and by which, therefore, the wagon rests upon it. The wagon is prevented from leaving the axle through a shock, by two wrought-iron flaps (Fig. 17) between which the bearing lies, and by a round bolt which goes through the flaps beneath the axle, and is fixed to them. The bearing consists of a plate 7¾ in. wide, 5 in. long, and 1 in. thick. On the upper side this is provided with a small projecting ledge, ½ in. high, and with two square holes through which pass the flaps, this firmly uniting the bearing with the frame timbers of the wagon. On the underside of the plate, between these holes, is a half-round seat, which rises 2½ in. from it, and is 4 in. long; so that the plate projects about 1 in. beyond the seat towards the side of the wheel. The flaps, with the screws for fastening them, are 14¾ in. long, and the lower part 3 in. wide. The bolts which lie under the axle are ½ in. diameter, which is thick enough as they are not required to carry any load but are employed only for the sake of security. Trials have shown that these cast-iron bearings have less

---

thick. The axles are turned from 2⅛ to 2⅛ in. in diameter, and are closely fitted in the holes; they are fastened with round pins which engage half in the axle and half in the nave, fastenings which appear to be very satisfactory. Curved spokes have been found unsuitable, as they made the wheels somewhat elastic. The turned parts of the axle are slightly longer than the bearings, so that the axle may move to and fro without the wagon sharing this motion. (*Footnote by Authors.*)

The railway to which the authors refer was the pioneer Continental public railway, recommended as early as 31 *March* 1808 *by Dr Franz Joseph Ritter von Gerstner* (1756–1832) *to link the rivers Danube and Moldau (now Vltava) along the old salt route. He was Professor of Mathematics, Mechanics, Art, and Philosophy at Prague University, and was unable to find time to pursue the idea. His son, Franz Anton Ritter von Gerstner* (1793–1840), *visited England in* 1822, *at the age of* 29, *to examine colliery railways, and later he secured a concession on* 7 *September* 1824 *from the Emperor Franz I granting him the exclusive right of building a Holz- und Eisenbahn (wood and iron road) between Mauthausen (on the Danube) and Budweis (on the Moldau). Budweis is now called České Budejovice. With the support of three Vienna banking houses, a company was formed under the title of 'k.k. privilegierte I österr. Eisenbahngesellschaft', and the first sod was turned on* 28 *July* 1825. *The first section, from Budweis to Trojanov, was opened on* 7 *September* 1827, *on a gauge of* 1·106 *m* (3 *ft* 7½ *in.*). *The line was extended to Kerschbaum on* 30 *September* 1828, *and passenger traffic was established. Shortly afterwards, von Gerstner junior retired from the undertaking in consequence of differences of opinion as to the methods of building and operating the railway. From the outset, both horse and bullock traction were employed, but Gerstner wished to introduce steam locomotion. This was the position at the time that Oeynhausen and Dechen were writing. Gerstner was replaced early in* 1829 *by Mathias Ritter von Schönerer* (1807–81), *who recommended diverting the route to Linz instead of Mauthausen. This course was adopted, and the line was opened through to Linz on* 1 *August* 1832. *Thereafter, it was commonly called the Linz–Budweis Railway. Animal traction was retained until* 12 *December* 1872.—*Ed.*

[1] *The original German text gives* 7½ *Sgr., possibly in error.—Ed.*

friction than brass, and that, with the wagon load of 50 to 60 cwt, they must be at least 4 in. long; smaller bearings cut slight furrows in the axle. The same bearings are employed also on the tipping-wagons, but the iron flaps are arranged differently; for this purpose they go straight downwards for 8 in., and then are bent outwards, so that the wagon cannot jump off the axle, and yet, without difficulty can be lifted.

To remedy the disadvantage of these bearings, namely, that the lubricant soon trickled off, the axles have been laid in cast-iron tubes, which are fixed to the wagon in like manner. These are provided with seats at both ends, by means of which they bear upon the axle; they have a lubricating hole at the middle. There are, however, no arrangements at the ends to prevent the escape of the lubricant, so that their object is attained only in part, and they have the disadvantage of increasing the weight of the wagon considerably. Only a few such wagons have been built, and no more will be made. Another kind of bearing is being tried, which promises more success. This consists of two parts. Fig. 18*a*, *b* is the upper part, which is fastened to the wagon frame by four screwbolts, the projecting lower ends of which serve also to fasten the underpart of the bearing, Fig. 19. These screwbolts are 1 in. square and are provided with a projecting collar which fits in a recess in the upper part of the bearing, and in this manner both parts are firmly united to the wagon. The whole length of the bearing is $9\frac{5}{8}$ in. In the middle is a chamber $1\frac{5}{8}$ in. long, which has a diameter of 4 in., while the axle has a diameter of only $2\frac{5}{8}$ in.; this chamber serves as an oil reservoir in which the lubricant can remain. On the upper side a lubricating hole is provided; the two side-parts, 4 in. long and 3 in. diameter, form the seats for the axle. The upper part of the bearing is flat on top, so as to fit firmly against the frame beam, Fig. 18*a*. The lower part is round underneath, to make it lighter. At both ends leather discs are placed, with the object of retaining the lubricant more satisfactorily.

The surfaces upon which the axle lies are chilled because a cast-iron mandrel is laid in the mould which quickly cools these surfaces. These bearings are not distinguished from the first because they are as long again, but because they are wholly enclosed underneath. The under part is cast as thin as possible, the iron being only from $\frac{1}{4}$ to $\frac{5}{16}$ in. thick, where it is not necessary, on account of the fastenings, to have a greater thickness.

These bearings are closely similar to those made in the workshops of G. Stephenson at Newcastle, and which, perhaps, are even more suitable for the purpose. They consist of only one cast-iron piece, which is similar to that in Fig. 18. The lubricating hole is in front, in the part of the bearing projecting beyond the frame, and leads in a sloping direction to the oil chamber in the middle; at both ends a pair of small recesses is turned out, wherein the closing leather discs are placed. The actual bearing surfaces are likewise chilled. On the underside, the axle is enclosed by a wooden half-bearing which fits entirely into the upper cast-iron piece, and is held fast by two wrought-iron bands. On the side faces of the wood, small iron plates covering the leather discs are screwed firmly. The cast-iron bearing, towards the wheel, has a ledge which projects beyond the leather disc, so that the nave of the wheel cannot rub against the disc. In the oil chamber there is a small iron ring on the axle, which serves for the better distribution of the lubricant. These bearings are lighter than those just now described, and may well conserve the oil still better, and therefore be preferred to them.

Arrangement of the Brakes for the Wheels

So as to be able to check the wagons or to retard their motion on those places on the railway where the wagons would run down by themselves, every wagon is provided with a brake which acts on the two wheels on the same side. This brake, Fig. 20*a*, *b*, consists of a wrought-iron lever which turns on a pivot mounted on the wagon midway between the wheel centres. To this iron lever is fastened a wooden block on which two cheek pieces of soft wood are fixed, so that, when the brake lever is depressed, these pieces bear against the two wheels on the same side of the wagon, the one above the centre and the other below, and thereby retard both these wheels. When the brake is not in use, its handle is placed in a ring or hook on the upper part of the wagon; while the brake is on, however, a man must press on the handle more or less heavily.

On the Darlington Railway, only this one kind of brake is employed; in other places, however, there are several kinds of brake to be described.

Wagons

Most of the wagons employed specifically for the transport of coal on this railway are of wood, and are painted with grey oil paint or black tar. Their dimensions are such that they contain 1 Newcastle chaldron, or 53 cwt; or perhaps 60 cwt when piled up.

One which was measured, was, in the clear, 6 ft 4 in. long at the top, 4 ft 8 in. wide, and 3 ft 4 in. deep; at the bottom, however, it was only 2 ft 7 in. long and 3 ft 2 in. wide. As the capacity is thereby so reduced, the 6 ft 4 in. long part of the wagon is made 10 in. deep by the addition of boards 7 in. high. From these measurements, the volume of this wagon is 85 cu. ft, or nearly 12 tons Pruss. (12,288 cu. in. Pruss.) and therefore can hold not more than 52 cwt of coal.[1]

They cost from £24 to £28 (168 to 196 thl.). In form and separate dimensions there are some unessential differences; one of the commonest wagons is shown in Fig. 21*a*, *b*, *c*.

These wagons consist of two frame beams 8 ft long, 4½ in. high, and 3½ in. thick, which are connected with one another by 4 cross-bars 3 ft 2 in. long, 3½ in. wide, and 2½ in. thick. To them the bearings for the axles are bolted, so that the centres of the wheels are 38½ in. apart. Upon the longer sides are four pillars 38¼ in. high, 2¾ in. wide, and 2 in. thick, tenoned into the frame beams, and these are connected at the top by a pair of beams 2½ in. square. The extra top boards are supported on these. On the short sides there are two pillars, mortised into the cross-bars above and below. The inside of this framework is covered with boards 1 in. thick. The upper and lower sidebeams are also connected by iron tie-bars. The ends of the frame beams are thickened with wood and are provided with iron sheaths; they are also fitted with the necessary hooks for yoking the horse.

An iron chain goes across the top of the wagon to give it more strength.

The whole bottom of the inner space, 2 ft 7 in. long and 3 ft 2 in. wide, forms a downward-opening door which hangs on two thick iron bars. These also have eyes at the side which are fixed through two little flaps hanging from the frame beam by two other eyes. Through the latter lies a cross-bolt which is fastened to a small chain. As soon as this bolt is withdrawn, and the flaps are lifted off their eyes, the door falls open and the load in the wagon pours out, partly by itself, and partly with a little assistance. The wagons are discharged on unloading stages, where the mass falls through openings in the railway on to the depot beneath. In a similar manner, these wagons are loaded at the collieries and limekilns.

There are also wagons on which the door is placed on one of the long sides; but these are found to be less durable.

At each end of the wagon, in the middle, a thick iron bar is screwed to two cross-bars and has a round hole at the end (Fig. 21*c*). These serve to couple the wagon with several others, for which purpose are employed the coupling piece, Fig. 22, which is 14 in. long; and the pin, Fig. 23. This method of coupling is much better than that produced by chains attached to the yoking hooks, as it forms a stiff connection between the wagons and prevent them from knocking against one another. This consideration is specially important for the wagon attendant, who often stands on one of the projecting beams between two wagons, and easily runs risk of injury when coupling chains are used.

[1] *Because of arithmetical difficulties, the translator suggests that the authors had in mind English measurements, despite their specific description as Prussian.—Ed.*

In order to connect and disconnect the wagons quickly from the rope on the inclined planes, the arrangement shown in Fig. 24*a*, *b* is employed. This consists of a wrought-iron coupling piece, which is fixed to the rope, and which ends with an iron chain (Fig. 24*a*). It is a kind of tongs, which engages with the last ring of the chain, and is fastened by a hook; it can open only when this hook releases it. The opening of the coupling takes place extraordinarily quickly; the hook is made free and the handle is turned downwards; whereby the under jaw of the tongs opens, the chain falls away from the rope, and the wagon is free.

In addition to the ordinary wagons for coal transport, as described, and those for lead in blocks, which consist only of the underframe, there are special tipping wagons for the building of the railway, and for its subsequent repair, which are distinguished by their fitness for the purpose. To enable material to be tipped between the rails, as is required daily to maintain the horse path by throwing gravel upon it, the wagon is provided with a door at one end; the opposite end of the wagon can be raised to a height. Beneath the wagon, a beam rests upon the axles, and is connected with them by two curved bars in which the axles can revolve. On the beam is a toothed iron bar passing through a cast-iron plate fixed to the wagon, and on this plate is mounted a small pinion which engages with the toothed bar and the axle of which can be turned by means of a crank put on it. When this is done, the wagon is raised and tipped. During the tipping, both axles and wheels remain standing on the railway, and the wagon rests with two bearings on one axle, while the two bearings, which are provided with the previously-described outwardly bent flaps, are lifted off the axle. Since the upright toothed bar is 4 ft long, the wagon can be placed in a steeply inclined position with little trouble.

Most of the lime wagons, also, are arranged in this manner. In these, the body is made of iron plate, because the lime is often hot when despatched.

The second kind of tipping wagon is used when it is desired to tip the material at the sides of the railway; this occurs specially with the construction of the railway, when embankments must be formed by degrees, by spreading around the easily-won earth from the cuttings. These consist of a frame formed of two beams and three cross-members. Upon this stand two low blocks, the tops of which are just above the tops of the wheels. These blocks carry two boxes 7 ft long, 3 ft 2 in. wide, and 1 ft 2 in. deep, which are attached to the blocks by a pair of brackets, so that they can be tipped outwards about pivots. At both ends of the frame stands an upright iron bar through which a cross-bolt can be put, by which the two boxes are held fast. The long outer side of each box forms a door which is hinged at the bottom, and is fastened by an iron bar in the middle and the corner posts at the top. For the discharge, these side doors are first opened, and the greater part of the contents can then be withdrawn with little trouble; the downward hanging doors protect the wheels of the wagon from damage. Then, after the cross-bolts are withdrawn, the boxes are tipped up and the remainder discharged. By reason of their small depth, the boxes are durable, although the whole side forms the door; with deeper wagon-boxes, this arrangement would not be suitable.

CAST-IRON RAILWAY FROM HETTON COLLIERY TO SUNDERLAND

General Remarks

In the neighbourhood of Hetton village, about 8 English miles ($1\frac{2}{3}$ Pruss. miles) from Sunderland, lies Hetton Colliery, at present the largest in England. This colliery has a chief establishment, called the *Lions pits*, $\frac{1}{4}$ mile from Hetton, and besides this, a smaller establishment, called *Elmore pits*, one English mile south of the first, is now about to begin production. At the chief establishment two seams are worked at a depth of 109 to 150 fathoms (654 and 900 ft Engl. or $95\frac{1}{4}$ and 131 fathoms Pruss.). Here are two large haulage pits, close to one another, 14 ft in diameter, which are partitioned off into several timbered compartments. Four 26-in. high-pressure steam winding engines raise the coal to the surface. On the surface a large and convenient discharging stage is built; the coal is discharged over sloping iron gratings through which the small coal falls; the larger coal arrives by the slope at the end of the grating where it is delivered directly through a shoot into the coal wagons. A wagon holds one Newcastle chaldron (53 cwt of 112 lb). The coal is then further transported on the railway next to be described.

In the neighbourhood of Sunderland a considerable amount of coalmining is undertaken. The chief part of this coal goes by the River Wear to London and to the east coast of England. For the commercial trade on the River Wear, in addition to the Hetton Colliery, the following collieries send coal:—

Lambton	Names of the owners
Russel	
Marq. Londonderry	
W. Stubbert	

These collieries have formed a combination, by which the quantity of coal to be raised is decided by a committee in accordance with the necessities of the market. The different interests are apportioned, not only yearly but also monthly, to which end a maximum output is fixed for each colliery.

In the year 1826, these collieries together sold not less than 517,746 Newcastle chaldron (27,440,538 cwt Engl.), or in Prussian weight 27,011,489 cwt or 6,752,872 tons Pruss.

The monthly output of Hetton Colliery at present amounts to about 8,000 chaldron of large and 2,000 chaldron of small coal; or, yearly, 96,000 chaldron (5,088,000 cwt) of large, 24,000 chaldron (1,272,000 cwt) of small coal, together totalling 120,000 chaldron (6,360,000 cwt) of coal. According to Prussian weight:—

Large coal	5,006,592 cwt
Small coal	1,251,648 „
Together	6,258,240 „

Calculating that 1 ton Pruss. = 4 cwt of coal, then the total output amounts to 1,564,560 tons Pruss., or $1\frac{1}{2}$ million tons in round numbers.

The coal is separated into different sorts which have different prices; these, according to the agreement of February 1827, delivered free on shipboard at Sunderland, are as follow:—

	1 Newcastle chaldron or 13 Prussian tons	1 Prussian ton
Hutton seam	36*s*. 6*d*. = 12 thl., 23 grs., 3 pfg.	29 grs., 5·7 pfg.
High main coal	30*s*. 6*d*. = 10 thl., 20 grs., 3 pfg.	24 grs., 7·6 pfg.
Low main coal	24s. 0*d*. = 8 thl., 12 grs., 0 pfg.	19 grs., 4·6 pfg.
Cambden main	16*s*. 0*d*. = 5 thl., 18 grs., 0 pfg.	12 grs., 11 pfg.
Nuts	12*s*. 0*d*. = 4 thl., 6 grs., 0 pfg.	9 grs., 8·3 pfg.
Small	9*s*. 0*d*. = 3 thl., 5 grs., 0 pfg.	7 grs., 3·7 pfg.
Dust[1]	6*s*. 0*d*. = 2 thl., 3 grs., 0 pfg.	4 grs., 10·1 pfg.

The first three kinds are the round coal from the three leading seams thus named; the fourth is poor soft round coal from the neighbourhood of the seam disturbance of these three seams; the last three sorts are mixed from the different seams; nuts are fragments which will not pass through a screen of ⅜ in. width; the last two kinds will pass through such a screen; the last is all dust-like, and is mixed with clay by brickmakers.

The mean price of the round coal can be reckoned at 33*s*. 6*d*., and for the small coal at 11*s*. per chaldron, according to which the yearly output of this colliery is worth £174,000 sterling, or 1,218,000 thl.

This enormous output appears still more astonishing when we take into consideration that it is procured from only two seams 6½ ft thick, and that it is raised to a single point, which, including the four winding engines, the discharge arrangement, the pumping engine, etc., does not occupy the area of a Prussian Morgen (180 square rods).

For this haulage, more than 5 million cwt must be brought 8 miles Engl. (1⅗ miles Pruss.) from the colliery to the depot and shipping place on the right bank of the River Wear above Sunderland. To facilitate this transport, and indeed to make it practicable, this great 8-mile long railway has been laid out.

General Description of the Railway

The rails are of cast-iron and have a gauge of 4 ft 7 in. (4 ft 9 in. Engl.). The line is led over the ridge of a substantial hill. The coal is hauled in chaldron wagons holding 1 Newcastle chaldron (53 cwt) partly by the help of stationary steam-engines, partly by steam locomotive engines, and partly by self-acting planes, with such speed, that, if necessary, and if losses of time at the different stages can be avoided, the whole distance of 8 miles can be covered in one hour; usually, however from 1½ to 2 hours are required, in which, at the same time the empty wagons are returned. The wagons are similar to those on the Darlington Railway.

This railway,[2] which, after the previously-described Darlington Railway, is the finest in England, occasioned a special interest on account of the considerable expenditure of mechanical power. On

[1] *Wrongly printed in the German text as 'Duts'.—Ed.*

[2] *The Hetton Colliery Railway was the first entirely new railway to be built by George Stephenson. He was invited in* 1819 *to undertake the work, and was allowed by his employers, the 'Grand Allies', to do this without any diminution in his Killingworth salary. His brother, Robert (after whom his famous son was named), was the resident engineer. The sinking of Hetton Colliery was begun on* 19 *December* 1820 *and the construction of the railway was taken in hand in March* 1821. *The line was opened with ceremony on* 18 *November* 1822, *when the first shipment of coal was effected by the Hetton Coal Company at its newly-erected staith on the banks of the River Wear. The railway passed into the ownership of the National Coal Board on* 1 *January* 1947. *After a working life of nearly* 137 *years, it carried traffic for the last time on Wednesday,* 9 *September* 1959, *and dismantling of the line was begun the next day. The last* 90 *ft of track at Hetton was removed on* 20 *November* 1960.—*Ed.*

a length of 8 miles, there are at work two locomotive engines, six stationary steam-engines, and five brake-arrangements on as many inclined planes. In addition, very convenient apparatus is built for discharging into ships, and a huge warehouse has been established close to the unloading place. With this large expenditure of mechanical power, which in the steam-engines alone amounts to 230 horsepower, it would be possible to haul 800 chaldrons (42,400 cwt) or 10,400 tons Pruss. of coal from the colliery to the staith near Sunderland in 15 hours, about double the quantity at present actually hauled. Whether this very considerable cost of construction and maintenance is justified by the intended achievement is a question which we hesitate to answer in the affirmative.

The railway is divided into several stages according to the nature of the ground. The different stages, their lengths, and their ascents, were communicated to us by Mr Forster, the viewer at Hetton Colliery, while we also measured the lengths by pacing (1 pace = 2·4 ft). The following is a summary thereof.

First Stage

From Hetton Colliery to near Rough Bank, or to the foot of the inclined plane, at the top of which is situated the first stationary engine, is 2,541 yards (7,623 ft Engl.) long, according to Mr Forster's statement. This forms a stage.

From Rough Bank to the shaft of the colliery there is a descent of 22 ft 9 in. Engl., or $\frac{1}{9\cdot 3}$ in. = 0·1042 in. per yard which is $\frac{1}{334}$ of the length, or an angle of 10 min. 17 sec. On this stage there are two steam locomotive engines with 9-in. cylinders, which draw up 16 loaded chaldron wagons at a time. In 14 hours each of these engines can make 24 journeys and haul 384 chaldrons (20,352 cwt), and even more if necessary. Their ordinary speed is from 4 to 4½ or 5 miles an hour, or 5·6 to 7 ft Pruss. per second, with either full or empty wagons. The arrangement of these locomotive engines is the same as those on the Killingworth Colliery Railway, with the two axles connected by a chain. With an annual output of 6 million cwt, and 300 working days in the year, this amounts to 20,000 cwt to be hauled daily, so that one locomotive engine would have to take 10,000 cwt, or to make 12 journeys; two locomotive engines are therefore more than sufficient to haul this amount.

Second Stage

The second stage is the inclined plane, at the top of which is a stationary engine of about 60 horsepower known as the Byre engine. According to our pacing, the length of this stage is 2,592 ft; according to Mr Forster's statement, however, the length is 832 yards (or 2,496 ft Engl.). On this length there is an ascent of 154½ ft Engl., therefore 2·23 in. per yard or $\frac{1}{16}$ of the length, which corresponds to an angle of 3°.32′.56″.

Eight loaded chaldron wagons are drawn to the top at a time, at a speed of about 3 miles an hour (about 4·4 ft per second). The rope to which these wagons are fastened has a circumference of 7¼ in. (2⅓ in. diameter) and should last 30 weeks. Eight loaded chaldron wagons is a load of about 600 cwt.

Third Stage

The third stage consists also of an inclined plane, extending from the end of the second stage to the Warden Law engine, a high-pressure engine of some 30 horsepower and with a pressure of 28 lb. The length of this stage we found by pacing to be 2,304 ft. According to Mr Forster's statement, the length is 775 yards (2,325 ft Engl.) and its ascent is 25 ft 6 in., therefore 0·4 in. per yard, or $\frac{1}{91}$ of the length, which corresponds to an angle of 0°.37′.51″. Here, likewise, eight laden wagons are drawn to the top, at about the same speed as on the previous stage.

Fourth Stage

The fourth stage reaches from the top of the former one to the top of the hill ridge. Here there is an ordinary-pressure stationary steam-engine of 60 horsepower. It is really two engines placed close to one another, each of 30 in. diameter, which work a common rope drum. Eight laden chaldron wagons are drawn together to the top, at a speed of about 3 miles an hour, on a rope having a circumference of 7¼ in., and which should last about 35 weeks. The length of this stage we found by pacing to be 2,112 ft; according to Mr Forster's statement it is 775 yards (2,325 ft Engl.), and the ascent is 115 ft, therefore 1·8 in. per yard or $\frac{1}{20\cdot 2}$ of the length, which equals an angle of 2°.50′.6″.

With this stage, the top of the hill ridge is reached. The whole length of the line from the shaft of the Hetton Colliery up to this point amounts to:—

	According to our pacing: Length in (Pruss.) feet	According to Mr Forster's statement: Length in (Engl.) feet	Height in feet	Ascent	Angle of ascent
1st stage	7,623	7,623	22 ft 9 in.	$\frac{1}{334}$	0°.10′.17″
2nd stage	2,592	2,496	154 ft 6 in.	$\frac{1}{16\cdot 1}$	3°.32′.56″
3rd stage	2,304	2,304[1]	25 ft 6 in.	$\frac{1}{91}$	0°.37′.51″
4th stage	2,112	2,325	115 ft 0 in.	$\frac{1}{20\cdot 2}$	2°.20′. 6″
Total		14,748	317 ft 9 in.		

The whole length is therefore about 2·8 miles Engl. or 14,342 ft. Pruss. = 2,151·3 fathoms Pruss.; the ascent thereon is 317 ft 9 in. This length is divided into four stages, upon which work three stationary engines and two steam locomotive engines.

From the top of the hill ridge to the staith on the bank of the River Wear, according to Mr Forster's statement, is a length of 8,819 yards (26,457 ft Engl.), or very closely 5 miles, therefore 25,692·4 ft Pruss. = 3,853·8 fathoms Pruss.; according to our pacing, however, this length amounted only to 25,539 ft Pruss.

This length is divided into seven stages, which fall continuously towards the staith. These descents are:—

5th stage	130 ft 4 in. Engl. fall
6th stage	129 ft 6 in. „ „
7th stage	54 ft 7 in. „ „
8th stage	76 ft 5 in. „ „
9th and 10th stages	63 ft 5 in. „ „
11th stage	67 ft 9 in. „ „
Total	522 ft

Therefore the bank of the shaft is situated 203 ft 4 in. above the depositing place, and the total descent of the line amounts only to $\frac{1}{202}$ or 0°.17′.12″.

Five inclined or self-acting planes and three stationary steam-engines convey the wagons down this part of the railway.

[1] *This figure differs from the one given in the text under 'Third Stage', but is consistent with the total of* 14,748 *ft given in the table.—Ed.*

Fifth, Sixth, Seventh, and Eighth Stages

Four inclined planes following one another form as many stages. Together they have a fall of 390 ft 10 in. Engl., and, according to Forster, a length of 4,144 yards (12,432 ft Engl., 12,072·7 ft Pruss., 1,811 fathoms Pruss.). According to our pacings, however, the length was only 11,514 ft Pruss.

The details according to Mr Forster are:—

	Length of (Engl.) feet	Descent in (Engl.) feet	Descent per yard	Fraction of the length	Angle of the descent
5th stage	3,906	130 ft 4 in.	$1\frac{3}{16}$ in.	$\frac{1}{30}$	1°.54′.43″
6th stage	3,672	129 ft 6 in.	$1\frac{1}{4}$ in.	$\frac{1}{28\cdot5}$	2°. 1′.33″
7th stage	2,148	54 ft 7 in.	$\frac{9}{16}$ in.	$\frac{1}{39\cdot8}$	1°.27′.23″
8th stage	2,706	76 ft 5 in.	1 in.	$\frac{1}{36}$	1°.37′ 6″
Total	12,432	390 ft 10 in.			

On the fifth stage is a rope of 5 in. circumference which lasts about 36 weeks; on the sixth stage a similar rope which lasts 59 weeks; and on the seventh stage a rope of $4\frac{1}{2}$ in. circumference which lasts a year.

Upon all of these inclined planes eight laden chaldron wagons, holding 53 cwt respectively, are let down at one time, and as many empty wagons are drawn up. This can be done at a speed of at least 10 miles Engl. an hour, or 14 ft Pruss. per second.

The total length of the railway over the hill ridge from the end of the first stage to the end of the eighth stage is 19,578 ft Engl., or 19,012 ft Pruss. = 2,852 fathoms Pruss. The total fall on this length is only 95 ft 10 in., or $\frac{1}{204}$ which corresponds to an angle of 0°.16′.49″. Had a tunnel been driven through the hill ridge, three stationary steam-engines and five self-acting planes would have been saved, and the most suitable inclination for the railway would have been secured.

Ninth and Tenth Stages

Stages nine and ten, according to Mr Forster's statement, together have a length of 4,350 yards (13,050 ft Engl.). The length of 2,602 yards, next the inclined planes, has a fall of $\frac{5}{16}$ in. per yard, $\frac{1}{115}$ of the length, or an angle of 0°.29′.23″, and the remainder, 1,748 yards, is nearly horizontal. The total fall of the two stages is 63 ft 5 in.

Three steam locomotive engines ran formerly on these two stages. In 14 hours a locomotive could haul 160, or the three together 480 chaldron wagons. A locomotive drew 16 laden wagons downwards and as many empty wagons back. A locomotive engine therefore covered the foregoing length of 4,350 yards 10 times forward and 10 times backward, and generally, in 14 hours, covered a distance of 87,000 yards (or, in an hour, 6,215 yards, or $3\frac{1}{2}$ miles), inclusive of all interruptions. It was found, however, that the railway was affected very injuriously by the locomotive haulage, and it is now preferred to draw the wagons forward and backward by stationary steam-engines. For this purpose the length of 4,350 yards is divided into two stages. The length of the first, or ninth, stage we found by pacing to be 7,500 ft, or about 2,500 yards, and that of the lower, or tenth, stage 1,850 yards. At the ends of these two stages there are three high-pressure steam-engines of 17 in. diameter, and 28 lb steam pressure to the square inch, which, by means of long ropes wound on drums, draw the full wagons downwards and the empty wagons upwards. The arrangement is such that the drums hang down from the engine, and then the wound rope is drawn out by the train of descending wagons; it is then wound back again with a new train of ascending wagons. Where the railway crosses a highroad, a trench is made in which runs the hauling rope; the trench is covered with a trapdoor. An attendant is stationed nearby, who, when the wagon-train approaches, opens the trapdoor, and closes it again when the wagons have passed. The hauling rope runs upon iron sheaves, which are placed at suitable distances.

On the upper stage 16 loaded wagons run regularly downward by their own weight, and are regulated by being braked a little. The mean speed is about 10 miles Engl. an hour, or 14 ft Pruss. per second. At about equal speed, the same number of empty wagons is drawn up by the steam-engine.

On the lower, or tenth, stage 24 laden chaldron wagons are hauled downwards by the lower engine, and the same number of empty wagons hauled back again, upwards, by the upper engine; this is accomplished at a speed of 10 miles an hour. We saw, however, 28 and even 30 wagons go forwards and backwards. On the upper stage lies a rope which is as long as the stage; on the lower stage, however, there is a rope twice as long as the stage, and this must be wound alternately on the drums of the engines at the two ends. The ropes on both stages are about $1\frac{1}{8}$ to $1\frac{1}{4}$ in. diameter.

Eleventh Stage

This stage is the last, and leads directly to the staith, where there is a large warehouse and very convenient arrangements for loading the coal directly into the ships.

The length of this stage is 325 yards or 975 ft Engl., and the fall is 67 ft 9 in. Engl., or $2\frac{1}{2}$ in. per yard, or $\frac{1}{14 \cdot 4}$ of the length, which corresponds to an angle of $3°.59'.4''$. On this self-acting plane, eight laden chaldron wagons are let down by the brake, on a rope of 7 in. circumference, and the same number of empty wagons is drawn upwards simultaneously. Such a rope lasts about 33 weeks.

Construction of the Railway

As already stated, the railway has a gauge of 4 ft 7 in. Pruss. (4 ft 9 in. Engl.); and is composed of cast-iron rails 3 ft $7\frac{1}{2}$ in. Pruss. (3 ft 9 in. Engl.) long, exclusive of the overlap. This lap is $2\frac{1}{4}$ in. long, so that the whole length of a rail is 3 ft $9\frac{3}{4}$ in. Pruss. (Fig. 25*a*, *b*, *c*). The rails are cast by Losh of Newcastle, who holds a Patent for them. The upper width is $2\frac{1}{2}$ in., and the corners are rounded off; the height of this part is $\frac{3}{4}$ in., and slopes underneath until it meets the strengthening rib, which is $\frac{7}{12}$ in. thick, and which terminates below in a round swelling $1\frac{3}{8}$ in. diameter. The end laps are $3\frac{1}{2}$ in. high and are on the alternate sides of the rail; they are somewhat tapered towards their ends. The greatest height of the rail is 6 in. in the middle. The laps are provided with round holes, by means of which they are fastened to the chairs.

The rails rest in cast-iron chairs (Fig. 26*a*, *b*), in which the two overlapping ends are fixed by iron pins. These chairs differ from the ordinary ones only in that their inner surface is rounded, so that the rail ends rest on a circular support, which should prevent the rails from being displaced if the chairs become tilted by the sinking of the earth. The intended objective is not wholly achieved by this means.

These chairs are small; their base is $4\frac{1}{2}$ in. long, $3\frac{1}{2}$ in. wide, and $\frac{3}{4}$ in. thick; the side plates are $2\frac{1}{4}$ in. high, $2\frac{1}{4}$ in. wide, and stand $1\frac{3}{4}$ in. from one another. Like those previously described in detail, these chairs are fixed to the stone sleepers by wooden plugs.

In addition to the rope sheaves already described on the Darlington Railway, many other kinds are employed on the Hetton, as on other early railways, partly on the ordinary straight lines, partly on curves or in sidings.

Where the inclined planes have curves, which is frequently the case on the Hetton Railway, guiding rollers are placed in the windings of the curves. These are fixed to wooden sleepers in the middle of the track, and are so inclined as to suit the degree of curvature and the gradients of the railway. They have the usual rope sheave construction; they are 7 in. diameter in the middle, with 2½ in. wide projecting edges; the breadth is 4¼ in., and their wrought-iron axles are 7 in. long. The lower end lies in a small iron bearing fixed on the principal sleeper; the upper end is held by a strong curved piece of cast-iron.

At the beginning and end of a siding there are usually longer guiding rollers; these are also of cast-iron and run upon wrought-iron axles, which rest in bearings similar to those of the sheaves. These are 21 in. long, 10½ in. diameter in the middle, and are arc-shaped towards the ends, to a diameter of 15 in., where they are provided with four arms which have a triangular cross-section.

At places where curves are to be followed, or where the descent of the wagons changes sharply, bell-shaped guiding rollers are employed, which run on wrought-iron vertical spindles, and are set, sometimes with the wide and open side upwards and sometimes reversed. These rollers are 16 in. high and 18 in. diameter at the open end, where they are provided with four arms of triangular cross-section; the diameter is sometimes decreased to 8 in. and finishes in a globe-shape. They are cast in very thin iron, and the thickness for the greatest part is not much over ½ in. Similar rollers are also given a barrel shape, composed of two truncated cones fastened together; this form is 15½ in. high, 7 in. diameter at the end, and 11 in. diameter in the middle. Others are in the shape of pots or cylinders 12 in. high and 10 in. diameter, which are provided at the base with a projecting rim 1 in. wide. The last are usually preferred in the sidings, where two such rollers are placed close to one another, and the rope passes between them.

Arrangement for attaching the wagons

In order to attach the wagons to the rope at the stationary steam-engines and the self-acting planes, and to be able to disconnect them easily, a curved wrought-iron bar is employed (Fig. 27*a*, *b*). To the top of the bar is bolted a strong 2 ft-long wooden cross-bar which leans aganst the end of the wagon; the attaching point for the rope is below the wagon body. The curved iron bar is connected with the coupling bar underneath the wagon by a vertical bolt (compare Fig. 21*c*). On the rope is an iron fork (Fig. 28), which is connected with the lower end of the curved bar by a horizontal bolt and linchpin. This bolt is knocked out with a wooden hammer, after the linchpin has been withdrawn, and the wagon thus released from the rope. This arrangement, however, is not so satisfactory as that used on the Darlington Railway.

Arrangement of the Sidings, and Braking Methods on the Inclined Planes

In the siding, there is usually a long guide-roller situated in the middle of the track, and also two upright cylindrical rollers, to lead the rope. Moreover, to make the movement of the wagons more certain, two beams 11 ft long and 4½ in. square, and with their ends shod with iron, are placed on the track, turning on pivots. These guide-beams prevent the full down-going wagons from slipping off the track, but let the empty wagons go upwards unhindered, because they push these timbers sideways.

At the middle of the inclined planes there is a siding, which, like most sidings, is from 270 to 300 ft long, and is constructed in the manner already described.

Between the two inclined planes there is a stretch from 420 to 480 ft long, upon which the line is quite or nearly level, so that the wagons can stand on it.

In the middle of this, close below the rails, lies the horizontal brake-wheel, the diameter of which is equal to the gauge of the railway, 4 ft 7 in. Pruss.

The sidings are constructed on this nearly horizontal part of the line, in the middle of which lies the brake wheel. The lower part of the railway on each self-acting plane consists of a single track, but the upper part has two tracks with a common central line, so that here there are three lines of rails lying 4 ft 7 in. Pruss., from one another, which is necessary on account of the course of the rope. Below the point where the wagons pass one another there are never two ropes, so here there is only one track; above these points, however, there are always two ropes, and, for that reason, there must be two tracks. Since wagons can never meet on this part of the line, a common central rail can be used. The brake wheel lies exactly in the middle; it is of cast-iron and has a groove for the rope. It appears that the rope is laid only once round the wheel; it is not clear how this prevents the rope from slipping when the wheel is braked, but it seems probable that a single turn of the rope on the wheel is sufficient. For each inclined plane there is a man who manages the braking of the wheel. The brake wheel lies covered underneath the line, some inches deep in a small chamber fitted up to receive it, so that, from the last guide roller, the rope runs underground. The mechanism for the brake-arrangement is also underground. The middle siding, in which the brake wheel lies, is normally employed, but is used only when it is desired to dispose of wagons without interrupting the haulage, as happens occasionally. On all inclined planes where the full wagons going down draw up the empty wagons, the upper half consists of three and the lower half of two single lines of rail, which on the first form two tracks and on the latter one track.

On stages 9 and 10, where the wagons are drawn by stationary steam-engines, no sidings in the stages are necessary, since only one train at a time is being worked. Near the engine houses there are sidings 540 ft long, because here the full and empty wagons interchange.

The wagons employed on this railway are similar in all their parts to those which were described on the Darlington Railway, so that there remains nothing further to remark about them.

Unloading Machine on the Coal Staith on the River Wear near Sunderland

The banks of the River Wear near Sunderland are very steep and almost perpendicular, more than 50 ft deep; between them and the river there is only a small level space.

The depth of water in the river is considerable, so that ships of substantial tonnage can come conveniently close to the bank. The railway from Hetton, and from the other collieries hauling to this place, comes down the valley slope some 50 or 60 ft by a self-acting plane, and ends 30 or 40 ft above the surface of the river. The machines for loading the coal into the ships are built at the end of this railway, close to the bank.

Although these have different arrangements, they agree with one another in essentials. By such machine, a loaded wagon that has come down the railway is lowered vertically until it is directly over the ship, and the coal is discharged by opening the door in the bottom of the wagon. During its descent, the loaded wagon draws to the top a counterweight, which raises the empty wagon back to the level of the railway. For loading the coal out of the covered warehouse into the ships, the same wagons and the same loading machine are used.

Three of these machines are distinguished by the ingenuity of their entire arrangement, and therefore merit a more precise description. The simplest of these (Fig. 30*a*, *b*) consists of a lifting-frame 36 ft high, at the base of which is a wooden axle 18 or 19 ft long, and 1 ft square, turning in iron bearings provided with caps. The main beams of the frame are 8 to 10 in. square; these are strengthened by struts and cross-bars. At the upper end of this frame there is an iron axle 3 or 4 in. thick, on which, by means of four iron bars 1 in. thick, is hung a platform which swings on the axle like a balance scale. This platform consists of a strong timber frame 8⅓ ft long on which a railway is laid. When the lifting-frame is upright, this platform hangs against the end of a railway laid on a stage and reaching as far as this point, so that the rails on the platform form a continuation of those on the adjacent stage. This platform can be fixed to the railway by means of a clamp, so that a wagon can proceed on to it; in front of the wagon lies a cross-beam, and behind it is placed a stop-beam to secure it against slipping off the platform. The lifting-frame is now let down by a contrivance and describes a large arc. The wagon on the platform is thus lowered upright on to the ship. A man who stands by the wagon opens the door in the base, the coal falls into the hold of the ship, and the platform, with the empty wagon, then ascends to the railway, so that the wagon can be removed. The arrangement for lowering and raising the lifting-frame is erected over the end of the railway. On the iron axle, on which the platform hangs, there are two cast-iron rope sheaves wherein lies a flat rope, one end of which is fixed to the stage. The other end leads over a guide roller to two sheaves upon a cast-iron (10 in. diameter) axle, on which there are also two small rope sheaves for the counterweight, and a large cog-wheel with 124 teeth and $7\frac{1}{2}$ in. across. This wheel engages with a small pinion with 28 teeth, on the axle of which a brake-wheel is fitted. The brake-wheel is of cast-iron, 8 ft in diameter, covered with a wooden sheath, around which is a wooden brake embracing about $\frac{5}{8}$ of the circumference. The counterweight consists of a chain, on which weights are hung at suitable distances. When the lifting-frame is upright, these weights rest upon the bottom of a small pit, and are therefore not in operation; as soon as the lifting-frame is lowered, and the overweight of the full wagon becomes greater, the weights are raised from the bottom of the pit and increase the mass of the counterweight. Thus, the brake has little to do, as the wagon and the counterweight continue in the same proportion, and the brake has only to carry the overweight necessary for the movement of the frame and wagon. When the loaded wagon is emptied, its weight of over 70 cwt is reduced to 18 or 20 cwt, which is overbalanced by the counterweight, so that the lifting-frame and the wagon are drawn again to the top. During this operation the counterweight is being lessened as the different parts of the weight are deposited at the bottom of the pit. By this arrangement, the wagon has a movement of 31 ft horizontally, and 26 ft vertically.

The second of the arrangements in many ways resembles the first. This consists of a long lifting-frame constructed in good truss-work, the upper arm of which is 38 ft long, and the bottom 19 ft long, which is placed on a strong wooden axle turning in iron bands. On the upper end of this frame there are two iron sheaves, over which flat ropes run, one end of which is fastened to a cross-beam of the stage. The other ends of these ropes pass over two guiding rollers to a rope drum where they are wound on two bobbins. On the same axle there are two brake-wheels with wooden brakes, the lever for which is on the discharging stage so that the workman can operate it from that situation. In the middle, between the two brake-wheels, there is a conical drum upon which a counterweight is wound, when the lifting-frame with the full wagon is let down.

By winding on a conical barrel, the radius at which the counterweight acts increases as the lifting-frame sinks, or becomes proportionately heavier. When the coal wagon is emptied into the boat, both wagon and lifting-frame are raised back to the top by the counterweight; the effect of the weight is reduced in the same proportion, and therefore little power is required for the raising. The platform on which the coal wagons are placed for discharging is exactly like that already described. When the full wagon is being pushed on to the platform, the latter is secured to the stage by two iron clamps; the second cross-beam is then turned, and fixed by projecting pegs, so that the wagon cannot fall off.

The weight of the lifting-frame itself is balanced in all positions by a counterweight acting on its lower end.

Immediately in front of this discharging stage, there is a self-acting plane, on which the wagons are likewise retarded on their descent by a counterweight, and the empty wagons then drawn back by it.

The height of the self-acting plane is about 25 ft, which is the height of the covered depot in which the coal is stored if it cannot be shipped immediately. The brake-wheel is on a drum on which runs a rope by which the wagon is let down. The rope on which the counterweight acts is wound on another part of the same drum. So as to reduce the travel of the counterweight, the other end of this rope is fastened to the stage and led over a guide-roller. The weight hangs on a loose roller, in a flat groove, so that the rope must be wound through twice the distance that the counterweight moves.

With this very convenient unloading arrangement, two men can ship 6 keels = 48 chaldron, or 2,544 cwt, in one hour; therefore, in 12 hours of working time they can deal with 576 chaldrons (30,529 cwt = 7,488 tons Engl. or 624 tons Pruss.).[1]

The third arrangement differs more from the other two; it is, likewise, a lifting-frame, the upper arm of which is 24 ft long, and the lower member 15 ft. The upper arrangement of the platform is closely similar to that of the machines previously described. At the lower end there is a very considerable counterweight, which properly balances, as far as is necessary, not only the lifting-frame but also the loaded wagon, at every point in the descent; and is in a position to raise the empty wagon back to the top. Underneath, on the lifting-frame, there are two toothed quadrants, formed of separate pieces of cast-iron fixed together, which engage with two small pinions mounted on an axle. On the axle there is also a brake-wheel, by which the velocity of the lifting-frame is determined, at both the raising and the lowering. Furthermore, to enable the lifting-frame to be brought to each position, there is a large toothed wheel on the axle, in which a small pinion engages and on the axle of which there are two winch handles. This arrangement is situated under the stage on which the end of the railway lies, in a roofed space; thus, only the lifting-frame, moving to and fro, can be seen from outside.

Besides these arrangements, there are others on the River Wear, not far from Sunderland, which serve to load into the large seagoing vessels the coal that is brought down the river in one-chaldron receptacles on flat keels. These are very suitable for such purpose. The arrangement consists of a double lever about 48 ft long, constructed of strong timber, and turning about a horizontal pivot at the middle. On both ends are iron rope pulleys over which a flat rope runs, the rope leading from the upper pulley to a drum which is housed in a small building containing a small steam-engine. At the middle of the lever there is a drum 10 ft diameter, round which a chain passes and is then led to the engine house, where it passes round a controlling brake drum; alternatively the chain may be wound on a drum connected with the steam-engine, so that by it the whole lever can receive a turning movement. The flat keel carrying the coal that is to be transhipped, lies between the river bank and the large ship.

At the beginning of the transhipment, the lever stands nearly upright with the lower end a little towards the front. The one-chaldron receptacle of coal is lifted off the keel to the end of the lever by means of the rope and the steam-engine; the lever is then turned, by the pull on the rope, so that the lower end, which stands over the keel, is raised, and at the same time stretches out further over the river. Thereby the coal receptacle is brought vertically over the ship, and is lowered by slackening the rope. The coal is then tipped out, the empty receptacle is drawn to the top, and the lever is returned to its former position, so that the receptacle can be lowered on to the keel and another laden one fastened to the rope, whereupon the operation is repeated.

[1] *The figures in parentheses are as given in the German text. The translator suggested their amendment to* 1,562 *tons English or* 7,632 *tons Prussian.—Ed.*

GREAT RAILWAY FROM LIVERPOOL TO MANCHESTER

The large traffic between Liverpool and Manchester suggested, several years ago, the idea of joining these two large trading and manufacturing places by a railway.

The advantageous results which the Darlington Railway afforded, has caused this idea to be revived more recently, and, by consent of Parliament,[1] a company has been formed which has subscribed a sum of £500,000 (3,500,000 thl.) for carrying out this undertaking. The workmen, under the guidance of Mr Stephenson, the builder of the Darlington Railway, began the construction in the neighbourhood of Liverpool in 1826.

As we saw the railway in April 1827, a beginning had hardly been made; the following description, therefore, must be restricted in general to what has been first carried out.

The country between Liverpool and Manchester, and the projects which have been made for the railway line, are shown on the first copper plate. The distance between the two cities is about 31 miles Engl. (6½ miles Pruss.). The line marked No. I is that first proposed by Mr Rennie of London; it goes in a northerly direction past St Helens and Newton, and its highest point lies only 101 ft Engl., above the level of Vauxhall Road near Liverpool. This point is in the neighbourhood of St Helens, and it follows from this that the ascent, when distributed over the great length, is very moderate. This line also afforded the advantage that it could be brought to the Mersey above ground, so that, without question, this scheme would have been the most suitable that could be proposed. However, the strong opposition met with in Parliament from the landowners necessitated the abandonment of this scheme, and the choice of another less suitable for the purpose. The new line authorised by Parliament goes between Prescot and Whiston, above Newton, and has already given occasion for various alterations of the plans. This line, marked No. II on the copperplate, is the last chosen by G. Stephenson, and will serve the general purpose.

As the course of the line which could be chosen was restricted, the length will amount to nearly 31 miles Engl.

The line, upon which work has now been begun, goes from Edgehill near Liverpool. On the way to Manchester it will have a generally advantageous country through which to cut, excepting at the Sankey valley, west of Newton, and at Chat Moss, a very swampy place between Newton and Manchester. The railway cannot be carried over these two places without considerable expense. From Edgehill to the bank of the Mersey the railway must be brought through the City of Liverpool, and, because the acquisition of the surface and the houses standing on it would be expensive, and also because it would be generally impracticable to carry on a frequent railway service in a crowded city quarter among heavy traffic of people and vehicles of all sorts, so it is intended here to carry the railway underground through a tunnel. Work on the railway was inaugurated in 1826 with the preparation of this tunnel. It begins somewhat above Lord Street, Edgehill, and ends somewhat below where Upper Pitt Street crosses Cornwallis Street; in the vicinity of Kent Street. The whole length of the tunnel is 1,996 yards, or 5,988 ft Engl. = 5,814 ft Pruss., or 872 fathoms Pruss., and on this length it has a fall of 121 ft Engl., which amounts to nearly ¾ in. per yard, or $\frac{1}{49 \cdot 5}$, or an

[1] *Act* 7 *George IV, cap.* 49, 5 *May* 1826.—*Ed.*

angle of 1°.9′.28″. The railway emerges from the tunnel to daylight, and is continued in an open cutting more than 150 yards, or 450 ft; it terminates at Queensdock, on the bank of the Mersey.

For the construction of the tunnel seven shafts are necessary, which are situated 10 to 15 yards (40[1] to 45 ft Engl.) to the side of it, and are to be kept open until the completion of the work. We entered shaft No. 5, which to the bottom of the tunnel is 21 yards (63 ft Engl. = 9·2 fathoms Pruss.) deep; it is constructed in brick walling. The walling on the longer side has a width of 12 in., and that of the shorter side is 4 in.; in the clear, the greatest length is 10 ft 8 in., and the breadth 8 ft Engl.

The tunnel is driven through soft red sandstone [belonging to the new red sandstone formation], the side walls of which promise to be stable; therefore only the roof is built in brickwork. The height of the tunnel is 16 ft Engl. in the clear. The brickwork begins at a height of 5 ft above the base, is formed to an arc of 11 ft radius, and is 18 in. thick. To build this, sections are driven 18 ft high and 25 ft wide. The width of the section at the base is 22 ft Engl., in the clear, and is more than sufficient for a double railway. The cost of driving one yard of tunnel is £7 1*s.* 0*d.* (49 thl. 10 grs. 6 pfg.), and, including the brickwork and all other expenses, the total cost comes to about £15 (105 thl.) a yard. The 1,996 yards of tunnel therefore costs about £29,940, and 150 yards of open cutting, cut at £5 a yard, costs £750, together totalling £30,690 (214,830 thl.). To carry the spoil more conveniently to the shafts, through which it is despatched to the surface, a temporary railway is laid in the section and follows the work.

The railway itself will be laid with wrought-iron rails, similar to those on the Darlington Railway. The rails are manufactured at many ironworks in Staffordshire, e.g. B. Bradley Ironworks, Forster and Co., near Stourbridge; in South Wales, at Penydarran Ironworks, near Merthyr Tydwill; in Northumberland, at Bedlington Ironworks, near Morpeth.

The wrought-iron rails, Fig. 31*a*, *b*, are of an improved form to those employed on the Darlington Railway. They are usually delivered in bars of 15 ft Engl. long, which are divided into 5 sections each of 3 ft Engl., or 1 yard. On the round-edged face the top is from $2\frac{1}{4}$ to $2\frac{3}{8}$ in. wide; the height of the rail at the ends, and at the separating divisions, is $2\frac{1}{4}$ to $2\frac{1}{2}$ in.; and in the middle, where the under-swelling is of greatest height, it reaches $3\frac{1}{4}$ to $3\frac{1}{2}$ in. The weight of these rails is 35 lb a yard; therefore 7 lb more than those on the Darlington Railway. This stronger rail is doubtless used because of the employment of steam locomotive engines, for which the rails on the Darlington Railway are somewhat too weak, and also to give greater security with a very large volume of traffic. For the freight-wagons, which weigh from 70 to 80 cwt inclusive, the lighter rails appear to be sufficient. The head of the rail is $\frac{3}{4}$ in. thick, and is provided underneath with a strengthening rib $\frac{3}{4}$ in. thick. The under-swelling is not equal on the two sides; at the chair points, it is absent altogether on one side and is $\frac{1}{2}$ in. high on the other. Where the rail is deepest, the swelling is 1 in. high on one side and $1\frac{1}{2}$ in. on the other. At each division of the rail there is a straight piece 5 in. long. The thickness of the swelling is 1 in. The weight of a running fathom of a single track of this rail is 154·71 lb Pruss., or of a Prussian mile of 24,000 ft is $5{,}063\frac{3}{8}$ cwt Pruss.

The fastening of these rails is disposed in a still more suitable manner than the wedge fastening used on the Darlington Railway. The cast-iron chairs, Fig. 32 and 33, therefore have a special form. The chairs which lie under the four intermediate points of the rail are different from those under the joints of two rails. Their size is almost equal; the base is $6\frac{3}{4}$ in. long, $4\frac{1}{2}$ in. wide, and 1 in. thick; the side plates are $1\frac{1}{2}$ to $1\frac{3}{4}$ in. high. On the inner flat face of one sideplate, a groove $\frac{1}{2}$ in. high and $\frac{1}{4}$ in. deep is provided, in which lies the tightening key for fastening the rail. The other inner face of the chair is employed to support the rail, Fig. 33, and is likewise provided with a groove $\frac{1}{2}$ in. high and $\frac{7}{8}$ in. deep, going right across the face, wherein fits the projecting ridge at the bottom

[1] *This figure appears in the German text; it may be a misprint for* 30.—*Ed.*

of the rail-web; this ridge is 5 in. long, $\frac{1}{2}$ in. high, and $\frac{7}{8}$ in. wide. In the joint chairs, however, Fig. 32*d*, this groove is only $2\frac{1}{2}$ in. long. So that the rail may fit into this recess, the $\frac{1}{2}$ in.-high ridge at the lower edge of the rail-web is cut away for a length of $1\frac{1}{4}$ in., at a distance of $1\frac{1}{4}$ in. from the end of the rail; thus a sort of shoulder stands out which can enter the recess. The connection of the separate rails is, of course, furthered by this means. One such cast-iron chair weighs 10 lb; the keys are made of hard iron, or still better of steel, in order that they may cut into the wrought-iron rails. The chairs will be laid on dressed stones, 2 ft square and 1 ft high. For fastening them, two holes are bored in each stone, in which wooden pegs are driven.

It will not be out of place here to describe the method of rolling these rails. We saw the rolls for the manufacture of these rails, Fig. 34, at the *Pen-y-daran* Ironworks, near Merthyr Tydwill, but not set up, and the drawing is made from the measurements taken of the rails, from the sight of the rolls, and from the verbal information obtained.

The rail to be rolled is $1\frac{5}{8}+\frac{3}{4}$ in., or $2\frac{3}{8}$ in. wide at the top, and its depth is $3\frac{1}{2}$ in. at the highest, and $2\frac{1}{2}$ in. at the lowest point; the whole length is 15 ft, divided into five equal parts 3 ft long. In order to roll this rail, therefore, a 15 ft long bar is taken, the width of which is $\frac{2\frac{1}{2}+3\frac{1}{2}}{2} = 3$ in., and the height of which is $\frac{1\frac{5}{8}+\frac{3}{4}}{2} = 1\frac{3}{16}$ in. This bar is either made by another roll, or by the rail roll, in a groove having these dimensions. When the bar is brought to the dimensions of 3 in. by $1\frac{3}{16}$ in., it must still be so hot that it can be run through the rolls six times to transform it into a rail.

The bar is admitted first to groove No. I, by which it attains a trapezoidal section 3 in. high by $1\frac{5}{8}$ in. and $\frac{3}{4}$ in. wide. It then enters groove No. II, where a somewhat rounded head is formed. In groove No. III the rounding is taken further and a projecting ledge is formed on one side at the lower end; in groove No. IV the head gets its full form and a projecting ledge is formed on the other side; the height of the rail remains unchanged at 3 in. In groove No. V, which the rail now enters, the swelling[1] is formed, and this is achieved by means of an excentric groove. As the rise of the curve amounts to 1 in., a ring is cut into the roll, the centre of which is $\frac{1}{2}$ in. away from the centre of the roll. Thereby, as the rolls turn, the height of the space No. V is sometimes $3\frac{1}{2}$ in., sometimes only $2\frac{1}{2}$ in. high, and, as the rail must follow this variation, an arc-shaped swelling is formed on its underside.

In the construction of the excentric groove, it has to be taken into consideration that the whole length of the piece of rail on which the arc-shape is to be put is 36 in. long. Also, when R = the radius of the excentric, $2R\pi = 36$ in., therefore $R = \frac{36}{2\pi} = 5{\cdot}75$ in., and so the radius of the excentric circle must be made $5\frac{3}{4}$ in. It remains to be considered that the underside of the rail must be straight for a length of 5 in. and only $2\frac{1}{2}$ in. high; therefore, on the excentric, an arc of 5 in. long must be struck from the centre of the roll and not from the centre of the excentric. The desired shape of rail results from the excentric groove so constructed. As the shape of the rail has not yet attained perfect sharpness during this operation, it is passed through the groove No. VI which provides the complete cross section of the rail at its highest point of $3\frac{1}{2}$ in. With this the operation is completed. It follows from this that these rails can be supplied cheaply only where puddling furnaces and rolling mills are in a flourishing condition; where these do not exist, laying out such railways cannot be considered. These rails are no dearer than the ordinary bar iron supplied by the rolls, and, according to the weight, their cost is only inconsiderably higher than that of cast-iron; because they need not pass through the rolls more often than as stated, and have only a slightly greater waste.

The gauge of the railway is 4 ft 8 in. Engl., or 4 ft $6\frac{3}{8}$ in. Pruss., and a double line will be laid for

[1] *Fishbelly.—Ed.*

the traffic. If the undertaking proves to be profitable, the laying of four tracks is contemplated, namely, one double line for the heavy traffic, and another for the rapid forwarding of coaches and travelling vehicles.

In April 1827 one ton (20 cwt) of wrought-iron rails, delivered in Liverpool, cost £13 10*s*. 0*d*. (94 thl. 15 grs.); for the chairs, 1 lb of cast-iron costs 1½*d*. (1¼ grs.), or £13 (91 thl.) a ton.

For consideration of these prices, reference may be made to what has been remarked about them already. It is necessary to add that, in December 1828, these rails are delivered at Newcastle from the Bedlington Ironworks for £13 5*s*. 0*d*., or 92 thl. 22 grs. 6 pfg., a ton, but the cast-iron chairs are supplied for £12 10*s*. 0*d*., or 87 thl. 15 grs. a ton. According to this, 1 cwt Pruss. of rail costs 4 thl. 21 grs. 5 pfg., and 1 cwt of cast-iron chairs costs 4 thl. 13 grs. 5 pfg.

On this railway, steam locomotive engines will perform the haulage; and stationary steam-engines will be erected at the inclines.

According to the published statement, the chief items of expenditure for this railway scheme appear to be estimated as follow:—

(1)	31 miles, of 1,760 yards, with four lines of rail, gives 218,240 yards of rail, at 35 lb a yard, amounting to 3,410 tons of iron at £13 10*s*. 0d.	£46,035
(2)	Upon 218,240 yards, one 10-lb chair a yard, or 975 tons at £13 a ton	12,675
(3)	A bridge over the Sankey valley	70,000
(4)	1,996 yards of tunnel at £15, and 150 yards of cutting at £5..	30,690
(5)	30 miles length of good road prepared for the railway at £1,500 a mile	45,000
	Total	£204,400

or 1,430,800 thl. This, for a Prussian mile, amounts to not less than 220,000 thl.

The projected bridge over the Sankey valley will be built of brick. The plan, which may undergo some alteration during its execution, is generally as follows. The bridge has twenty pointed arches, through the highest of which the Sankey Canal passes in the bottom of the valley. The height of the railway above the canal is 72 ft Engl. The span of an arch is 40 ft Engl., and the height 36½ ft. These rest on piers 8 ft wide. The spandrels are hollow, but a flat arch on which a thin brick wall is built is placed at the four points immediately under the rails. The arches are 5½ to 6 ft thick. From the arch through which the canal passes, there are 13 arches on one side and six on the other, totalling 19 arches. These at 40 ft, with 20 piers at 8 ft, and two half-arches at the ends, have a total length of 960 ft Engl., or 320 yards. At one end of this bridge the level of the railway is 50 ft Engl. above the ground, and at the other end 37½ ft, to which heights embankments must be thrown up with the help of retaining walls.

RAILWAY FROM BOLTON-LE-MOORS TO LEIGH

Near the Liverpool & Manchester Railway is another railway, which at present is being laid out under the direction of Mr Edgeworth from Bolton-le-Moors to Leigh, a distance of about 7 miles ($1\frac{1}{2}$ miles Pruss., or 5,383 fathoms Pruss.), and doubtless in future will be extended to that railway. The chief purpose of this railway is the transport of coal from the region of Leigh to Bolton; and also the transport of merchandise by the various canal connections between Liverpool and Manchester and Leigh, thus conveniently providing the very populous and industrial region of Bolton with provisions of all kinds from Ireland. A stock company[1] has subscribed £40,000 (280,000 thl.) for laying out the line, but it may be asked whether all the expenditure can be covered by this sum.

Since it is designed to join this railway with the great Liverpool & Manchester Railway, it is laid to the same gauge of 4 ft 8 in. Engl., and has wrought-iron rails of exactly the same sort as on that line. The ground over which this railway passes is very uneven, so that at least two, and possibly three, stationary steam-engines will be necessary in order to convey the wagons upwards or downwards.

In 1826 the workmen began marking out and levelling the line between Bolton and Chakubent (*probably meaning Chequerbent*); between Chakubent and Leigh, however, the line of the railway was not at the time (April 1827) quite settled.

From Bolton the line is nearly horizontal for a length of about 600 yards; then an ascent begins, at first with a slope of $\frac{1}{30}$, or an angle of $1^\circ.54\frac{1}{2}'$, and then at $\frac{1}{50}$, or an angle of $1^\circ.8\frac{1}{3}'$. The length of these severe ascents is about 1 mile Engl. (1,760 yards or 769 fathoms Pruss.), and at the end of this second division of the way a stationary steam engine will draw up or let down a train of wagons.

The third stage has only a small ascent on a short length, by which the highest point on the railway is reached, about 150 ft Engl., above Bolton. From this division point, as far as an isolated tavern near Chakubent on the road from Bolton to Wigan, the line falls very little, with a slope of $\frac{1}{360}$ or an angle of $9\frac{1}{2}$ min. The length of this third stage is about 2 miles Engl. (3,520 yards or 1,538 fathoms Pruss.); locomotive engines will be used on this without the help of stationary steam-engines.

The fourth stage comprises the descent of the hill ridge towards Leigh; this is 2 miles Engl. long and has a vertical height of 290 ft Engl. The upper end of this descent is at $\frac{1}{30}$ or an angle of $1^\circ.54\frac{1}{2}'$; and the lower part at $\frac{1}{60}$, or an angle of $57\frac{1}{4}$ min. For this reason, it will be necessary to erect a stationary steam-engine at the upper end of this stage, near Chakubent, with which to haul up or let down a train of wagons by an endless rope, according to Mr R. Edgeworth's proposal. Mr G. Stephenson is certainly of opinion that this arrangement would be practicable on the very considerable length of 2 miles Engl. (1,538 fathoms Pruss.); in the meantime, another plan is being considered which divides this stage into two separate parts, with a sharper descent, and with a

[1] *Incorporated as the Bolton & Leigh Railway Company by Act of* 6 *George IV*, *cap.* 18, 31 *March* 1825. *The line was opened for goods traffic on* 1 *August* 1828. *The connecting link from Leigh to the Liverpool & Manchester Railway at Kenyon was authorised by an Act of* 14 *May* 1829.—*Ed.*

nearly horizontal part between them. Then, however, a third steam-engine would become necessary, at the upper end of the second inclined plane.

The fifth stage extends to Leigh and is 2,860 yards long. Like the first stage, it is nearly level and either steam locomotive engines or horses can be employed here.

The earthworks between Bolton and Chakubent are being built at the present time. At one place it is necessary to raise an embankment up to 20 ft high and at another to cut 26 ft deep; this involves a considerable cost. The earthwork is 17 ft wide at the base. Only a single line will be laid, and sidings will be built where necessary.

The earth won in the cuttings is used for filling, and for this purpose a temporary railway is laid on wooden planks. This consists of wrought-iron bars 1 in. wide and 2 in. high which are fixed in cast-iron chairs; the end pieces in the sidings are of cast-iron. The wagons employed on building this railway are arranged so that they can be tipped easily. On the middle of the wooden frame there is a small cast-iron pedestal, upon the top of which the sheet-iron wagon body rests. The body turns on trunnions fixed to the pedestals; it is fastened to the frame by a chain so that it cannot tip up while travelling. At the short side of the wagon there is a door which hangs on a round iron bar that ties together the tops of the side walls. The door is fastened at the bottom by a hook, against which a spring presses, so that it may be opened easily.

The approximate line of this railway is indicated on the map of the country between Liverpool and Manchester (Plate I). The short distance from Leigh to the larger railway amounts only to 2 miles Engl. A connecting railway would have a length of about $2\frac{5}{8}$ miles Engl. or 4,620 yards or 2,019 fathoms Pruss.; and the capital for laying it out is already raised. Moreover, the construction of a branch[1] from the main line between Liverpool and Manchester to Warrington has been decided upon; it will lead from Newton to that place.

Another plan is being developed which may have far reaching consequences for the whole internal traffic of England. By this it is desired to join by a railway 32 miles Engl. long ($6\frac{3}{4}$ miles Pruss.) the Peak Forest Canal on the west side of Derbyshire with the Cromford Canal on the south-east side of the hilly part of Derbyshire. The railway would meet the Peak Forest Canal near Whaley Bridge[2] and from here it is planned to carry the line further by Stockport to Manchester. Thereby, a continuous railway connection would reach from Liverpool by Manchester, Stockport, and Whaley Bridge, to the Cromford Canal. This plan is very complicated and will need to overcome many hindrances to its construction; the scheme has already been worked on by J. Jessop in 1824.[3] The country through which the railway between the Cromford and Peak Forest canals would pass has very steep valleys and considerable heights, since various points on the route lie about 1,000 ft Engl. above the Cromford Canal. The different stages of the line are approximately as follow:—

About $\frac{1}{2}$ mile Engl. from Cromford, the railway begins with a self-acting plane with a perpendicular height of 465 ft Engl.; leading with an arched bridge over the road between Cromford and Wirksworth, and proceeds by a short level stretch to Middleton Cross, where a second self-acting plane, of 265 ft ascent, raises the line again. Then the route goes horizontally to the foot of the third self-acting plane, which is 60 to 70 ft high and is $3\frac{1}{2}$ miles Engl. from the beginning of the railway. The line thus reaches a height of 800 ft above the starting-point and can continue at this altitude for a length of nearly 12 miles Engl., crossing the Ashbourne, Bakewell, and the Manchester

---

[1] *Parliamentary approval had not been obtained at the period in which the authors were writing. The Warrington & Newton Railway Company was incorporated by an Act of* 10 *George IV, cap.* 37, 14 *May* 1829.—*Ed.*

[2] *The German text gives Wayley Bridge.—Ed.*

[3] *The Cromford & High Peak Railway Company was incorporated by Act of* 2 *May* 1825 (6 *Geo. IV, cap.* 30). *The engineer was Josias Jessop* (1781–1826), *a son of the famous William Jessop* (1745–1814). *The* $15\frac{1}{2}$*-mile section from Cromford Wharf to Hurdlow was opened on* 29 *May* 1830, *and the line completed for the remaining* $17\frac{1}{2}$ *miles through to Whaley Bridge on* 6 *July* 1831.—*Ed.*

roads. Here a tunnel 1,440 yards long will be necessary to save a separate self-acting plane. Near the Monegash and Hartington roads, the greatest altitude of the railway will be reached by a fourth self-acting plane; this height is 1,000 ft above the Cromford Canal and 760 ft above the Peak Forest Canal near Whaley.[1] If it had been decided to use a separate self-acting plane instead of the tunnel, then that fifth inclined plane would have been near Hurdlow. Both the self-acting plane and the long tunnel might have been avoided if the line had been given an ascent of $\frac{1}{11}$ in. a yard or $\frac{1}{396}$, for a length of 3½ miles Engl., and a cutting 24 ft deep had been made at the summit of the hill. From here the line extends for 3½ to 4 miles through a rough hilly region. Near Edge End lies the highest part of the watershed, 1,140 ft above the Cromford Canal, which is formed of so sharp a hill-ridge that 140 ft can be cut from the height by means of a tunnel 1,500 ft long. The line reaches its greatest height near to the Goyt road, and continues for 11¼ miles. Here it falls with a first self-acting plane of 460 ft into the valley of the Goyt. Then it goes along the valley slope, until it crosses the Manchester road near Ferneylee, and then descends with a second-self acting plane of 265 ft into the valley falls near Horridge. From this point up to the canal near Whaley Bridge there is a fall of 45 ft in a distance of 1,100 yards, which length is surmounted, partly by a third self-acting plane, and partly by a continuation of the canal, the supply pool of which lies 15 ft higher than the foot of the incline.

The great detour that this railway makes is unavoidable by reason of the hilly country. Nevertheless, the line is so chosen that there is a continuous ascent from both ends to the highest point.

According to an approximate estimate, an English mile costs £4,000 (28,000 thl.); therefore the whole length would cost £128,000 (896,000 thl.).

The line is divided equally into nearly horizontal parts and into steep ascents. On the former, horses and steam locomotive engines can work; on the latter, stationary steam-engines.

Approximate Income from the Railway

	Tons		£	Thaler
(1) Beverages	40,000	going 30 miles at 2 pence per ton-mile	10,000	70,000
(2) Coal	60,000	„ 10 „ „ 1 „ „ „	2,500	17,500
(3) Lime and Limestone	10,000	„ 8 „ „ 1 „ „ „	333	2,331
(4) Plaster and Proof-stone	10,000	„ 30 „ „ 1 „ „ „	1,280	8,960
(5) Hopton Wood stone (slab-forming sandstone)	5,000	„ 20 „ „ 1 „ „ „	465	3,255
(6) Cast-iron, bar-iron and plate	4,000	„ 30 „ „ 1 „ „ „	500	3,500
(7) Building timber, hay	1,000	„ 30 „ „ 1 „ „ „	125	875
(8) Wool and Cotton	2,000	„ 30 „ „ 2 „ „ „	500	3,500
(9) Goods to Manchester	2,000	„ 30 „ „ 2 „ „ „	500	3,500
(10) Goods from Manchester	5,000	„ 30 „ „ 2 „ „ „	1,250	8,750
(11) Goods from and to Huddersfield, Yorkshire	1,000	„ 30 „ „ 2 „ „ „	250	1,750
(12) Special Beverages	1,000	„ 30 „ „ 2 „ „ „	250	1,750
(13) Other objects	3,000	„ 30 „ „ 2 „ „ „	750	5,250
		Total	18,676[2]	130,732[2]
Deduct the working expenses of 32 English miles of railway at £30 a mile		£960		
Expenses of administration and other costs		£1040 Together	2,000	14,000
		Total	16,676	116,732

[1] *Here the German text uses the familiar English spelling of Whaley.—Ed.*

[2] *These totals are as given in the German text; they are only approximately correct, and may represent the effect of 'rounding off' some of the items in the original computation. The columns as here set out total £18,703 and 130,921 thaler.—Ed.*

An estimate of the probable traffic upon such a railway can be only approximate, says Mr Jessop in his report to the Committee. It is clear, however, that the connection between several well-established canals which form the trade-routes between the commercial districts of Lancashire, Derbyshire, and Nottinghamshire, between the southern and eastern agricultural districts—a connection which requires only a ¼ of the first cost of a canal—and which passes near valuable stone quarries and collieries, cannot fail to be profitable.

These receipts are the interest on a capital of £150,000 at 11 per cent. In addition to these tariff rates (which for 1 cwt a mile Pruss. are 2½ and 5 pfg.) payment must be made for the use of the stationary steam-engines and locomotive engines, which, considered collectively as freight charges, will not amount to 1*d*. a ton mile Engl. (2½ pfg. per cwt a mile Pruss.).

The separate costs in respect of building the railway are estimated as follow:—

	£	*s.*	*d*
(1) Laying out the ordinary way	2,319	19	0
(2) Cuttings and Embankments	17,015	10	8
(3) Retaining walls for Embankments	1,175	17	0
(4) Bridges and openings	1,633	10	0
(5) Tunnel near Burbage Edge	3,700	0	0
(6) Stonework	7,656	0	0
(7) Fencing	6,400	0	0
(8) Cast-iron rails	61,950	0	0
(9) Sleepers, spikes, and chairs	5,810	0	0
(10) Land acquisition	4,800	0	0
(11) Buildings and compensation	1,000	0	0
(12) Warehouses and depots	2,000	0	0
(13) Allowance for contingencies, covering the estimates at 10 per cent	11,746	0	0
Total	[1]129,206	16	8
Steam-engines, etc., for the inclined planes, of which there are at least six	20,000	0	0
Together	149,206	16	8

or 1,044,447 thl. 25 grs.

The cost of the locomotives for the level or slightly inclined parts of the line is estimated as follows: 1 locomotive engine of 10 horsepower will take 120 tons = 2,400 cwt at the ordinary speed of a horse, or 50 tons = 1,000 cwt, at a speed of 6 miles Engl. an hour. It requires one man and one boy for its attendance, which costs 5*s*. a day; from 20 to 30 cwt of coal is burned in 10 hours, so that the daily cost may be estimated at 30*s*. (10½ thl.). Therefore 1,000 cwt can be transported 60 miles Engl. (12½ miles Pruss.) in 10 hours. Although bringing back the empty wagons has to be reckoned in addition, it will be seen that the costs of carriage are inconsiderable.

Towards the Cromford Canal there are four inclined planes, and towards the Peak Forest Canal three planes; to transport 1 ton, of 20 cwt, over the line will cost about ½*d*.

[1] *This total is as given in the German text; the correct total of the individual items is £127,206 16s. 8d.—Ed.*

SHORT DESCRIPTION OF SOME OTHER RAILWAYS IN ENGLAND

A. ENGLISH RAILWAYS[1] OF CAST-IRON

I. Railway from Dartmoor to Plymouth

Dartmoor itself is a hilly region in Devonshire with an elevation up to 1,800 ft. The soil consisting mostly of bare granite hills, is little cultivated, except for excellent hewn stone and poor pasture.

In recent times, the granite building stone of Dartmoor, which is easy to win because it lies about mostly in large loose blocks, has been considered of special value for the great public buildings in London, the new London Bridge over the Thames, the breakwater at the entrance to Plymouth harbour, and the 5-arch bridge over the Cattewater,[2] near Plymouth, as well as at those places on Dartmoor where flying-bridges were built in a former age. To facilitate the use of this building stone, suitable arrangements must be made for transporting it overland for a distance of 12 miles Engl. (2½ miles Pruss.). Combined with this is a plan to make this barren country accessible and to cultivate it. In one of the most desolate regions of Dartmoor, a large building called a *Prison of War* has been built at the cost of the State. This was intended for the reception of those made prisoner in the last war,[3] but this became unnecessary with the establishment of peace, so that the building at present stands empty. In the year 1819, a company was formed with the object of sending poor children from London parishes to this *Prison of War*, to be instructed and to learn the manufacture of flax and stone cutting work. When grown up, they would be taught land cultivation. Previously, in connection with the plans of this company, the Dartmoor Railway Company had been formed in 1818 with shares of £50 (350 thl.). An Act of Parliament was passed in 1820[4] which authorised the company to lay an iron railway from the *Prison of War* to Crabtree, a length of about 12 miles Engl.; at the same time the Government was empowered to advance £18,000 (126,000 thl.) to the company in order to extend the railway from Crabtree along the seabay of Cattewater to Plymouth.

On 12 August 1819, the first rail was laid by Sir Th. Tyrwhitt, and the work proceeded quickly; the railway was finished successfully,[5] but the plan for the Dartmoor cultivation met with such great difficulties that it appears to be abandoned, at least for the present.

Thus, this costly scheme has missed at least one of its chief objects, and is scarcely able to bear the interest on the share capital, because it is restricted solely to the transport of stone. At the new turnpike on the road from Plymouth to Exeter, close by the Railway Inn, the railway divides into two branches. One leads to Sutton Pool, the harbour of Plymouth; the other runs on the right bank of the Cattewater to the large limestone quarry there.

The railway consists of cast-iron rails from 3 to 4 ft long, and has a gauge of 52½ in. Pruss. (54 in. Engl.). The rails rest in cast-iron chairs fixed on stone sleepers.

---

1 *The German text is 'Englische Schienenwege (Railroads)'.—Ed.*

2 *The German text gives 'Catwater'.—Ed.*

3 *The reference, of course, is to the Napoleonic War.—Ed.*

4 *The Act which incorporated the Plymouth & Dartmoor Railway Company* (59 *Geo. III, cap.* 115) *was passed on* 2 *July* 1819; *the Act of* 8 *July* 1820 (1 *Geo. IV, cap.* 54) *was for making a branch railway.—Ed.*

5 *The railway was opened from Sutton Pool, Plymouth, to King's Tor on Friday,* 26 *September* 1823; *it was extended to Princetown in October* 1826.—*Ed.*

They are similar to those on the Hetton Railway and likewise are cast according to Losh's Patent. The newer ones have the following arrangement; the laps at the ends are not on opposite sides as with the former, but on the same side of the rail. For that reason they are so laid on the line that with one rail the laps lie upon the outer side of the track, while those of the two adjacent rails lie on the inner side. The length of the rail, including the two laps is 46 in.; the lap is $2\frac{1}{2}$ in. long; therefore the running length of the rail is only $43\frac{1}{2}$ in. The upper width of the rail, on which the wagon-wheels run, is $1\frac{3}{4}$ in., and the height of this part is $1\frac{1}{4}$ in. It joins on to the lower strengthening rib, $\frac{3}{4}$ in. thick. The height of the laps is 4 in., and the greatest height of the rail in the middle is 6 in. The rib ends at the bottom in a round swelling $1\frac{1}{4}$ in. wide and 1 in. high. The laps are provided with a round hole, so that they can be fastened to the chair by a pin. The chairs at the bottom are 7 in. long and 5 in. wide; the holes for a proper fastening are $\frac{3}{4}$ in. square; the baseplate is 1 in. thick. The side walls are 3 in. high and just as wide. These chairs are at some points spiked to wooden sleepers, 3 in. thick, 6 in. wide, and 5 ft long. The older rails are without laps; have a length of only $34\frac{1}{2}$ in. Pruss. (3 ft Engl.), and butt together with straight ends. They rest in similar chairs to the first, and at each end have a semicircular notch through which goes the fastening pin. These rails are $1\frac{3}{4}$ in. wide at the top. They have a $\frac{3}{4}$ in. thick strengthening rib, which terminates below in a swelling $1\frac{3}{4}$ in. diameter; at the head the rib is $1\frac{1}{4}$ in. thick. The height of this rail is 4 in. at the ends, and 6 in. in the middle; the upper broad face is only $\frac{1}{2}$ in. thick. These rails do not appear to be fastened so securely and durably as those with overlapping end laps.

The line generally has a gentle fall, but at many places the down-going laden wagons must be braked; there appear to be no ingenious mechanical arrangements on these wagons. Those for the transport of large stones are very simple; they consist of two strong frame-beams 9 ft long, 6 in. high, and 3 in. wide, which are connected by cross-beams. The iron axle-seats lie in thick wooden blocks under the beams. The frame beams are covered with planks $2\frac{1}{2}$ in. thick, on which are laid iron bars $1\frac{3}{4}$ in. wide and $\frac{3}{4}$ in. thick, so forming a platform $8\frac{1}{2}$ ft long and $4\frac{2}{3}$ ft wide. Below the axle seats there are further iron bars which reach from one end of the wagon to the other. The cast-iron wheels turn on the axles. The naves are $8\frac{3}{4}$ in. long, 2 in. bore at the front end and $2\frac{1}{4}$ in. behind. The wheels are 29 in. diameter; the tread is $4\frac{1}{2}$ in. wide and conical, so that the diameter close to the flange is $29\frac{3}{4}$ in. The flange projects $1\frac{1}{2}$ in. and is $\frac{3}{4}$ in. thick. The wheels have nine spokes, $\frac{3}{4}$ in. thick and $4\frac{3}{4}$ in. wide. The wheel centres are $41\frac{1}{2}$ in. apart. The brakes are of a form very suitable for the purpose; they are of cast-iron and fixed to a long wooden lever which can turn about a pin on the wagon frame. The brake acts on both wheels at one side of the wagon, with a suitable arc having a chord 13 in. long from top to bottom; they are 2 in. wide. Frequently the wagons have a similar brake on both sides, so that all four wheels may be braked. The wagons are coupled by connecting links 15 in. long, exactly like those used on the Darlington Railway (Fig. 24). A suitable crane is employed to raise and load large stones weighing up to 80 cwt and more. This crane is mounted on a wagon as described above, and therefore may be brought easily to any place on the railway where it is required; in this it differs essentially from other cranes which are stationary. The arrangement briefly is as follows: On the wagon frame there is a fixed column 6 ft high and 1 ft diameter at the bottom, and about this the crane turns; the latter consists of a strong 10 or 12 in. wooden beam, sloping at an angle of 50°. On the upper end of this is the pulley over which is led the chain on which the load is hung. On the beam is screwed an iron frame carrying the winding drum and the double wheelwork whereby the power is increased 200 times. It is connected with a platform by several ties and struts, and, by means of six 5 in. high rollers, this rests upon a guide on the wagon, and also is provided with friction rollers inside, where the pillar goes through it. On that side towards which the main beam inclines, this platform is provided with a horizontal wooden frame which can be extended easily so that a counterweight can be put on it when the crane is required to lift a load.

A similar crane to that just described is employed at a large stone quarry near Whitehaven in Cumberland, which is used mainly in connection with the building of the harbour for that place. In addition, however, this has some useful arrangements which are not on the Dartmoor crane. The frame on which the crane rests lies wholly over the running wheels, and is necessarily wider than the gauge of the line; it is 7 ft and just as long. It consists of three frame-beams 8 in. high, which are connected by cross beams. At the four corners, strong iron screws go through the frame beams, and these are provided with nuts above and below the frame and at the bottom with plates, whereby the crane can stand on the ground. After it has gone to the point where it is needed, the crane is raised by these four screws so high that the wheels rise off the rails, and the rails cannot be damaged by the great load of the crane. In addition to these four main screws, there are four others which are provided with a hook at the bottom. Large stones are fastened on these by chains to give the crane more stability. A cast-iron pillar which is rounded at the top stands in the middle of the frame and forms the turning point of the crane. Upon this hangs a hollow cast-iron cylinder, closed at the top by a cover with a lubricating hole; the remainder of the wooden crane-frame is fitted on this. Through the lever and the post goes a wrought-iron bolt, provided at the top with a head and at the bottom with a screw and nut. This binds the crane not only to the fixed pillar but also to the wagon frame. The crane has a platform at the bottom, mounted on four iron wheels which run on a circular iron rail. This is united with a plank frame whereon the counterweight for the load is hung. In order to turn the crane there is a fixed cogged wheel on the wagon frame; a pinion mounted on the crane engages with the wheel, and is turned by a crank-handle by means of two bevel wheels.

The axle-bearings of the drum and the pinion wheel for moving the load are separately screwed on the wooden frame. There is a double wheel-train and an intermediate axle, so that, as the crank axle has two wheel-pairs which can be put out of gear, the power can be increased about 70 times or 250 times. The advantage of these movable cranes cannot fail to be appreciated on all railways where loads composed of one large piece require to be handled.

Since the laying out of the Dartmoor Railway was necessitated, at least in part, by the building of the great breakwater at Plymouth, a short notice of this great undertaking will be not wholly out of place here.

The Breakwater at Plymouth

The roadstead of Plymouth, namely Plymouth Sound and Cawsand Bay, although offering a fine and spacious anchorage, is very exposed, first to the southerly and southwesterly, and lastly to the easterly winds, which cause here an extraordinary pressure and surging of the waves, which upon this rocky, and in many places shallow, anchorage becomes highly dangerous. Plymouth Sound has, therefore, at all times, been held in bad reputation by English mariners, and the words of Lord Howe are remembered that 'This sound would one day be the grave of the British fleet'. The celebrated architects John Rennie and Joseph Whidbey, were therefore commissioned by the Admiralty to devise an expedient to hold off the pressure of the sea from Plymouth Sound. In their report of 21 April 1806, they proposed to achieve this object by building a great stone embankment (pier or breakwater) at the entrance to Plymouth Sound, and this plan was sanctioned in the name of the King on 12 January 1811 after careful consideration. The first stone of this important structure was laid as early as 12 August 1812. When completed, the whole length of this enormous embankment will amount to about 850 fathoms (5,100 ft Engl.), 4,953 ft. Pruss. = 743 fathoms Pruss. and its greatest height will be 63 ft Engl. (61 ft Pruss.).

It rises 3 ft above the highest flood point, and 18 ft above the lowest ebb; the greatest width amounts to 420 ft at the bottom and to 30 ft at the top. The slope towards the open sea is about 1:4, and towards the harbour 1:2. The cross-section, therefore, amounts to 14,175 sq. ft. Engl., and the cubic contents to 72,292,500 cu. ft. Engl. = 223,483 cubic fathoms Pruss. The embankment is built of huge stone blocks, obtained for the most part from the limestone quarry of Oreston near Cattewater, which provides a fine marble-like transition limestone. In addition to these, granite blocks from Dartmoor are used, especially for lining the upper parts of the embankment.

The costs of this great public building undertaking have been estimated by Rennie and Whidbey at £1,171,000 (8,197,000 thl.) as follow:—

Cost of the Breakwater

2,000,000 tons of limestone in blocks from 1½ to 2 tons weight, at 7*s*. 6*d*. a ton, for the embankment	£750,000
360,000 tons for the pier built out at Andarn Point at 7*s*. a ton	126,000
20 per cent for contingencies	175,200
Total	£1,051,200

Cost of a Pier and Lighthouse on the Breakwater, built of hewn stone

42,000 cubic yards of walling in the outer and inner walls of the pier at 27*s*. ..	£44,700
62,000 cubic yards of rubble between the outer and inner walls of the pier, at 6*s*.	18,600
Large stone blocks to pave the top of the pier, 8,500 square yards	22,950
Two lighthouses with reflectors and Argand lamps	5,000
20 per cent for contingencies	28,650
Total	£119,900

From 1812 to 1816 nearly a million tons of stone were used in the breakwater, namely from 12 August 1812 up to the end of:—

1812	16,045	tons (of 20 cwt)
1813	171,198	„
1814	239,480	„
1915	264,207	„
1816 up to 12 August	206,033	„
Total	896,963	tons

The size of the blocks employed comes to:—

From 1 ton and under, each stone ..	423,904	tons
„ 1 ton to 3 tons, each stone ..	309,706	„
„ 3 tons to 5 tons, „ „ ..	150,593	„
Over 5 tons	12,760	„

The greatest quantity of stone which was laid in a week amounted to 15,379 tons, and, at the end of this period, the part of the breakwater which had been raised 3 ft above the psring tide level and 30 ft wide, had a completed length of 360 ft. After this time, up to August 1820, the following quantities of stone were used:—

From 13 August 1816 to 12 August 1817	220,405	tons
„ „ „ 1817 „ „ „ 1818	169,219	„
„ „ „ 1818 „ „ „ 1819	225,460	„
„ „ „ 1819 „ „ „ 1820	228,852	„
Total	843,936	tons

The total amount of stone used in the building, from 1812 to 1819, amounted therefore to 1,740,899 tons of 20 cwt.

Since this time the building of the breakwater has been continued, although with less activity, and at present (1827) is not yet wholly complete, so that it is not yet possible to begin building the lighthouses.

For the transport of the larger masses of stone, 10 ships of 80 tons burden have been built in the Royal Dockyard. These ships can carry 16 blocks, each of 5 tons weight, in two rows, each block resting on a wagon which runs on a railway. The two railways on the ships are extended to the breakwater by drawbridges; and then the wagons are drawn out of the ships by cranes and unloaded.

In this manner, a ship of 80 tons can be unloaded in 40 or 50 minutes. The ships are brought to the place where the stones are required to be laid by the help of buoys, and the exact line of the breakwater is maintained by the observation of lights or rods erected on the shores.

For the transport of the small stones, 43 ships of about 50 tons burden were hired from private persons. These ships are unloaded by a crane in only about 3 hours.

Already, the success of this great undertaking has answered expectations completely. At the end of two years, when about 800 yards of the middle part of the breakwater first began to be visible at the lowest ebb tide, the pressure of the sea had become so well broken that the fishermen at the end of the Sound were no longer, as formerly, in a position to judge the state of the sea by the holding back of the inland waters. Since this time, about 200 sailing vessels have found shelter behind this breakwater in stormy weather. The adequate length it possesses offers a secure anchorage for about 25 to 30 men-of-war during all weathers.

Particularly in the exceptionally stormy winter of 1816–17 did this breakwater prove its value. On 19 January a hurricane arose such as the oldest sailors could not remember, and the tide rose 6 ft above the ordinary spring tide level.

The sloop *Jaspar* and the schooner *Telegraph*, which kept outside the shelter of the breakwater, were both driven up the Sound and wrecked; but a heavily laden coal ship, which lay in the shelter of the breakwater, kept out of the hurricane. It was the general opinion, from previous experience, that, if the breakwater had not been present, then all shipping in the Cattewater would have been lost, and the store and warehouse buildings of the victualling warehouse, and most of the buildings on the shore, would have been washed away.

II. Railway at the Clydach Colliery near Swansea

Clydach Colliery lies 5 miles Engl. north of Swansea, some distance from the canal[1] leading to that place. A well-constructed cast-iron railway 2½ miles Engl. (1,922 fathoms Pruss.) long leads from the canal to this colliery. As the colliery is considerably above the bottom of the valley, a self-acting plane about 150 yards long, and with a slope of 12 to 14°, serves to lower the coal; 2½ tons (50 cwt) of coal, in two wagons, is lowered with the aid of a brake in about 48 seconds. The railway is similar to those at Hetton and Dartmoor.

The single rail is 3 ft 6 in. long inclusive of the laps on one side; each lap is 2½ in. long, and the running length of a rail is therefore 3 ft 3½ in. The upper face is 2 in. wide and 1¼ in. high, but much rounded at the corners; the strengthening rib is 1 in. thick and at its lower edge for a height of ½ in. is 1½ in. thick. The laps are 4 in. high; the greatest height of the rail is 5¾ in. These rails are fixed in cast-iron chairs by transverse pins through the laps. The chairs have a baseplate 8 in. long, 3 in. wide, and 1¼ in. thick; the side-walls are 2¾ in. high. These chairs are fixed on stones which are dressed level only on a space large enough for the chair to rest, and are otherwise not faced. Holes are bored in the stones at a distance corresponding with the chair holes, and wooden plugs

[1] *The Swansea Canal, which was incorporated by Act of* 23 *May* 1794 (34 *Geo. III, cap.* 109) *and opened in October* 1798.—*Ed.*

are driven into them; the chair is then fixed thereon by two iron spikes about 4 in. long. The stones lie so deep that only about half the chairs projects above the ground. The gauge of this line is 3 ft 6 in. in the clear of the rails; it is intended for horse traction.

Fifty-two pieces of this rail weigh 1 ton or 2,240 lb; therefore a single one weighs 43 lb. The cost of 1 ton is £7 to £8 (49 to 56 thl.). A Prussian fathom of this railway weighs about 172 lb, and costs from 3 thl. 22 grs. to 4 thl. 8 grs., as 1 cwt of rail costs from 2 thl. 13½ grs. to 2 thl. 24 grs. An English mile of this railway has cost £1,000 (7,000 thl.); therefore one Prussian fathom costs 9 thl. 3 grs.

From the foot of the self-acting plane to the canal, the railway has a moderate descent. The wagons used on it hold about 1¼ tons (25 cwt) of coal. From such wagons (5 tons, or 100 cwt) are taken downwards by one horse, and likewise drawn back again empty. The wagons are about 35 in. wide, 31 in. high, and 65 in. long; some are built of iron plate, and others of wood. The latter are found to be more advantageous, as they are lighter. This performance of a horse seems very small as compared with that on the Darlington Railway, where one horse is able to draw even double the load, namely 200 cwt. Usually on the self-acting plane two or sometimes three such wagons are let down at the same time. They are attached to an iron chain which weighs 14 lb a yard and is about ½ in. thick.

The wheels of these wagons are of cast-iron, and are fastened by a wooden lining in the round nave, which is 5½ in. long, on to a wrought-iron axle 2¼ in. thick which goes right through the nave; a washer and linchpin are provided on the outside. These wheels are of 21 in. diameter and are 3½ in. wide; the flange stands out 2 in. and there are 10 spokes in the wheel. The upper part of the bearing is of cast-iron 3½ in. wide, and under the axle lies a curved piece of wrought-iron which is fastened to the upper part by the same bolts that fasten the latter to the wagon frame. The brake, by which the wagons are let down, has a drum about 9 to 10 ft long and 6 ft diameter. This has a cast-iron axle with trunnions of 5 to 6 in. diameter; on this are fixed six or seven cast-iron circles clothed round the circumference with boards. On one side of the drum there is a wooden brake wheel; the braking is done by means of an iron band which is pressed against half the circumference of the brake wheel.

III. Cast-Iron mine-tram frames at Whingill Colliery near Whitehaven

The Whingill Colliery, near Whitehaven in Cumberland, is one of the most important in the neighbourhood. The open tract of mining area near Whitehaven must be 40 or 50 miles Engl. (30,000 to 38,000 fathoms Pruss.) long, and the length of the iron rails lying therein is 10 miles Engl. (7,700 fathoms Pruss.). (*These approximate conversions accord with the original German text.—Ed.*)

The rails are of cast-iron, 4 ft Engl. long, of the usual kind as employed upon the Hetton, Dartmoor, and Clydach railways. A running foot of this rail, including the cast-iron chair, which rests on wooden sleepers, weighs 21 lb. One English mile of 5,280 ft therefore weighs 49½ tons, and 10 miles Engl., 495 tons or 9,900 cwt. Reckoning that a ton of these rails and chairs costs £9 or 63 thl. Pruss.; the railways at these mines cost £4,455 (or 31,185 thl.).

The wagons which run on these railways have a cast-iron frame consisting of two side plates connected by two wooden cross-bars 3 in. square. The upper part of the axle bearing is cast directly on the frame; the under part is screwed to it. The length of the side-plates is 45 in. at the top; they stand 21 in. apart. The wheel centres are 23 in. apart, and the gauge is 25 in. On this frame is placed an osier wickerwork basket, which is provided with an iron hoop-handle and bottom band, and holds 11 cwt of coal; this is used also as a shaft-hauling container. The wheels are 19 in. in diameter and have the following arrangement; the axles lie in bearings and both wheels are fixed on the axle so that they turn with it. As the railway cannot be kept very clean, and has many curves, which in the mines is unavoidable, this method has some disadvantages, brought to light during long continued haulage, but compensation may be made by its greater solidity. To retain so far as possible the advantages of the fixed wheel arrangement, one wheel has been fixed on the axle and the other wheel allowed to run loose; the loose wheels are placed diagonally opposite to one another. The fixed wheels have a round nave, which is driven on to the square pyramidal axle. A cotter goes through the axle and engages with the nave, enabling the wheel to be forced on the axle more and more. The axle is $1\frac{5}{8}$ in. thick. The wheel that turns upon it is suitably built; the nave is cast about 4 in. deep in front and is provided with a lubricating hole. On the axle is a welded-on collar, against the outer side of which the wheel lies when it is placed on the axle. On the other side of the collar, there is a cast-iron disc formed with a recess to accommodate the collar; this disc is screwed fast to the wheel and so prevents it from slipping off the axle. A cloth disc is placed in between so that the lubricating oil cannot escape. Such wheels are used on several German railways (*tramroads*). In order to reduce still more the friction of these wheels, and to make them more durable, they are fitted with bushes which are hardened inside and are provided with a recess at the middle to hold the oil better; this cavity is not hardened. On this railway one horse draws ten such wagons coupled together, laden with 110 cwt of coal, which is a very good load for mine haulage; in a day's work one horse will cover the distance of 1 mile Engl. (769 fathoms Pruss.) eight times and return just as often with the empty wagons. The haulage of one horse is therefore 880 cwt on a length of 769 fathoms Pruss. At the mine, 60 horses are employed continuously. The total haulage amounts to 6 million cwt yearly.

Round and broken coal costs: 1 ton of 20 cwt, 7*s*. 6*d*. to 7*s*. 11*d*., or 1 ton Pruss. of 4 bushels, 15 grs. 9 pfg. to $16\frac{1}{2}$ grs.

Slack, 1 ton of 20 cwt costs 4*s*. to 4*s*. 2*d*., or 1 ton Pruss. of 4 bushels, 8 grs. 5 pfg. to 8 grs. 9 pfg.

The greatest part of this coal is shipped to Dublin, where it has to pay an import duty of 2*s*. 6*d*. a ton (or 5 grs. 3 pfg. on 1 ton Pruss.).

IV. Railway from the Slate Quarry near Penrhyn to Port Penrhyn

Penrhyn, near Bangor in North Wales (Caernarvonshire), are important slate quarries which yield a very pleasing, thin-splitting slate. The quarries lie $6\frac{1}{4}$ miles Engl. ($1\frac{1}{3}$ miles Pruss.) from the sea at Port Penrhyn, and a cast-iron railway was laid in 1800 and 1801[1] to convey the slate thereto.

The country descends continuously from the quarries to the harbour. The line is divided into five stages; it falls $\frac{3}{8}$ in. a yard or $\frac{1}{96}$ (35′.48″) and has three self-acting planes. The railway is neither well laid nor specially well maintained, but is used only for the transport of slate, the loads of which cannot be very great, and involves no costly outlay.

The gauge of the railway is 24 in. The rails are 3 ft long, and differ from any of those previously described, but are of much poorer construction; the cross-section is an ellipse $1\frac{3}{4}$ in. high and $1\frac{1}{4}$ in. wide. At each end is a 4 in. long piece of the rail $2\frac{1}{4}$ in. high and at the bottom straight and $1\frac{3}{4}$ in. wide, which is inserted in a cast-iron chair. These chairs are 8 in. long, 6 in. wide, the baseplate is $1\frac{1}{4}$ in. thick, and the side walls are 1 in. high; they are joined by cast-iron cross-sleepers. The rails are not fixed very carefully into these; some are merely placed in, but others are fixed by spikes. The cross-sleepers rest on stone sleepers. In the quarry, however, where the railway must often be relaid or lengthened, the rails merely rest on wooden sleepers, in which they are either sunk, or fastened by spikes driven in on both sides of the rail.[2]

The wheels of the wagons which run on this railway have double flanges, which is very unsuitable; the wheels are 12 in. high, with a rim $2\frac{1}{4}$ in. wide; the nave is $3\frac{1}{2}$ in. long. The axles of the wagons themselves turn, and the wheels also turn on the axles.

[1] *Thomas Tredgold in 'A Practical Treatise on Rail-Roads and Carriages'* (1825) *states that this railway was begun in October* 1800 *and finished in July* 1801.—*Ed.*

[2] *An account of this railway was published in the 'Repertory of Arts and Manufactures', vol. III, 2nd Series* (1803), *page* 285. *It was 'Communicated by the Inventor, Mr. Benjamin Wyatt, of Lime Grove near Bangor'.—Ed.*

Wagons for the transport of the finished slates have only a wooden or iron railing standing up from the strong bottom of the wagon; they hold 1 ton, of 20 cwt of slates. In the quarry, tipping wagons with wooden frames are employed for carrying away the refuse. The wheels lie inside of a wooden frame upon which a small pedestal is erected; on this one half of the wagon body rests and is hung so that it may be turned. The other end of the body is held by a pair of sloping supports held fast by a cross-bar. As soon as this bar is withdrawn, the supports fall down; the wagon body becomes free on the pedestal and is then easily tipped over.

A more important railway than this, 10 miles Engl. long, leads from the slate quarry near Llanberis, between Bangor and Caernarvon, to the despatching place on the seashore.[1] The rails are 3 ft long and rest on iron cross-sleepers. They are 2 in. high and 1½ in. wide, not elliptical, but flat and wide on top and pointed underneath.

A similar sort of convex rail, only much thinner, is employed at the Halkyn lead mine near Holywell in Flintshire. It is provided at one end with a projection and at the other end with a cavity, the one fitting into the other. These rails are 3 ft long, 3 in. at the ends, 4 in. high in the middle, and 1 in. thick. They are therefore much better constructed than the preceding rails. At each end a plate 5 in. wide and 1 in. thick is cast on, which is provided with holes for fastening it to the sleeper, and the employment of separate cast-iron chairs is made superfluous.

We saw a trial rail, made according to this idea, at the office of the Liverpool & Manchester Railway; it was very heavy and hence would not be of any immediate use. This rail has a plate at one end which projects 2½ in., and there is a groove throughout the height of the rail; on the other end is a tongue ¾ in. thick and projecting 1¼ in. The plate is 5 in. long, 5 in. wide, and 1 in. thick. Without the plate, the rail is 2½ in. high at the end and 6¾ in. in the middle. The whole length of the rail is 4 ft. The width at the top is 2½ in.; the strengthening rib is 1 in. thick and increases at the bottom to 1½ in. Two square holes are formed through the tongue and the groove. These rails are very easy to lay, as they have no separate chairs; the plates on the rails are fixed directly to the sleepers. Also, the fastening of one rail under the other is a good arrangement.

V. Railway from Middleton Colliery to Leeds

This railway[2] serves partly to provide Leeds with coal, and ends in a very conveniently-arranged depot in the city itself. The railway has been mentioned already, as it is the only one upon which steam locomotives on Blenkinsop's arrangement are in use.

The line consists of the following stages:—

(1) From the foot of the Middleton self-acting plane to the beginning of the Hunslet self-acting plane, 5,253 ft long; fall 58 ft 11 in., $\frac{1}{89}$, or with an angle of 0°.38′.33″.

(2) Hunslet self-acting plane, 1,053 ft long; fall 60 ft, $\frac{1}{17\cdot5}$, or with an angle of 3°.16′.10″.

(3) From the foot of this plane up to the southern end of the coal depot at Leeds, 6,798 ft long; fall 26 ft 4 in., or $\frac{1}{260}$ which corresponds to an angle of 0°.13′.29″.

(4) Length of the coal depot 594 ft, wholly horizontal.

The whole length of the first three stages amounts to 13,104 ft Engl. = 12,725 ft Pruss., or 1,909 fathoms Pruss.

The cast-iron rails are 2½ ft, also indeed 3 ft long. They are 3 in. high at the ends and 6 in. in

[1] *This was the original Padarn Railway, from the Dinorwic Slate Quarries at Llanberis to Port Dinorwic. It was built in* 1824 *and was horse operated. An entirely new alignment between the quarries and the port was adopted in* 1848, *on the 4-ft. gauge, and was steam operated from then until the abandonment of the railway on* 27 *October* 1961.—*Ed.*

[2] *Also called Brandling's Railroad. It was built by Charles Brandling with the aid of an Act of* 9 *June* 1758 (31 *Geo. II, cap.* 22) *for establishing agreements made between himself and other landowners for laying down a Waggon Way. The track was re-laid for the inauguration of locomotive traction (mentioned earlier) in* 1812.—*Ed.*

the middle; the width at the top is 2 in. The strengthening rib is ¾ in. thick and 1½ in. wide at the bottom. These rails are without laps, and butt against one another in common chairs. Thus are the rails on one side of the track. On the other side the rails are provided with cogs which engage the toothed wheel of the locomotive. These rails are 3 ft long; they have an upper face 2 in. wide whereon run the carrying wheels of the engine; the teeth are on the outer side of the rails and are 2½ in. wide. The strengthening rib is 1½ in. thick and increases at the bottom to 2¼ in. The provision of teeth to one of the running rails is disadvantageous to the movement of the locomotive engine, since the motive power is not exercised on the middle but acts on one side only. On the other hand, this arrangement has the advantage that it makes possible the employment of horse haulage also on this line; in such circumstances a toothed rail in the middle of the track would be undesirable. The pedestals on which the toothed rails lie differ from the others in that they have only one straight side wall, and at the other side a pair of buttresses which engage directly under two rail teeth.

The weight of these rails is as follows:—

The simple rail per yard ..	40 lb
The chair	6 „
The toothed rail per yard ..	56 „
The chair	14 „
	116 lb

The price of the cast-iron rails is stated at 12*s.* per cwt or 4 thl. 6 grs. Pruss.; the price of the cast-iron chairs, 18*s.* 8*d.* per cwt, or 6 thl. 16 grs. Pruss.

Therefore 1 yard of this railway costs:—

In cast-iron	13*s.* 7½*d.*
2 stone sleepers ..	2*s.* 0*d.*
To lay 1 yard.. ..	7*d.*
	16*s.* 2½*d.*

or 5 thl. 22 grs. 4 pfg. Pruss.

The gauge is 4 ft. The wheels of the locomotive engine are 36 in. high. Very suitable arrangements are made at the coal depot. The wagons have doors in the bottom; the railway runs over masonry-vaulted arches, and in the middle of each vault there is an iron shoot, by means of which the coal is emptied into the separate compartments. Alternatively, the line runs on to a wooden frame; the space under this is made into separate compartments by several partition walls, and likewise by a middle wall, the upper part of which is formed as a flap, so that coal can be tipped into either side of the compartment. This has the advantage that the coal may be delivered out of both sides of this compartment.

The wagons hold 54 cwt of coal, namely 24 loads; 1 load = 3 bushels and 1 bushel = 84 lb.

A locomotive engine draws between 26 and 32 wagons on the stretches of the line above and below the Hunslet self-acting plane, upon a length of 2¼ miles Engl. The total load, therefore, amounts to 1,400 to 1,700 cwt, exclusive of the weight of the wagons, which, at 23 cwt a wagon, makes the whole weight of the wagons 600 to 736 cwt. The total load which the locomotive engine draws is therefore 2,000 to 2,436 cwt. The engine hauls this at a speed of 3·5 to 4·9 ft Pruss. per second. One of these locomotive engines makes six journeys daily and burns 40 cwt of coal.

The self-acting plane at Hunslet has an upright brake drum, and two lines of rails which cross at the upper and lower ends, so that the wagons from above and below can be brought on to either line, as desired; an arrangement which has many advantages. It will let down four wagons together by the brake.

The prices of coal at the Leeds depot are as follow:—

			1 ton Pruss.
24 loads best quality	..	16*s*.	.. 12 grs. 11 pfg.
„ „ second quality	..	14*s*.	.. 11 grs. 4 pfg.
„ „ small rich coal	..	12*s*.	.. 9 grs. 7 pfg.
„ „ slack	..	6*s*.	.. 4 grs. 8 pfg.

24 loads are very nearly 12 tons Pruss.

The simplest construction of cast-iron English rails is to be found on a railway which leads from the neighbouring coal and ironstone mines to Lowmoor Ironworks near Bradford (Yorkshire). The rails are 3 to 4 ft long, 3 in. wide, and 2 in. thick, and are provided at each end, on the outer side only, with a projecting piece having a hole through it by means of which the rail is fixed to the stone sleeper. The ends of the rails abut smoothly together.

This railway is similar to that which leads from the shaft of the Landore colliery to the Tawe Canal near Swansea. The rails are 2½ ft long, 2 in. thick, 2½ in. wide, and the outer corners are blunted. The rails overlap at the ends, and thus the two are fixed to the wooden sleeper with one spike. The inside gauge is 27 in. The fastening of these rails is, at least, more suitable for the purpose than that of the preceding line. This railway was out of use.

B. ENGLISH RAILWAYS[1] OF WROUGHT-IRON

We have already noticed larger railways of wrought-iron, like the Darlington, already completed, and that between Liverpool and Manchester, in course of construction. The following railways deserve mention by reason of their simple and light construction, and therefore their cheap cost of laying out, as being very useful for light haulage on the surface and in mines.

VI. Wrought-Iron Railway at the Peddenandrea Mine near Redruth

Near Redruth, in Cornwall, at the Peddenandrea mine, there is a very simple wrought-iron railway built of bar iron, which forms a branch of the larger railway to Perranwharf, the length of which, when completed, will amount to 11 or 12 miles Engl. (2⅓ to 2½ miles Pruss.). This railway leads also near the Consolidated Mines, passes east of Redruth, and is 4 miles Engl. from here to its end point at Perranwharf, where the ore and coal ships arrive from South Wales via Falmouth. This main line belongs to a separate company; the branch leading to the mine belongs to the mine itself.

The railway under consideration, at Peddenandrea mine, consists of wrought-iron bars 14 ft long, ¾ in. thick, and 2½ in. high. These rails rest in cast-iron chairs, in which they are secured by wedges. To enable these to be driven in better, small grooves are rolled in the rail, on both sides, ¼ in. wide and ⅛ in. deep, and situated ½ in. from the lower edge; the upper corners are somewhat rounded. The chairs have a base-plate 5 in. square and ½ in. thick; the side walls, which are quite smooth inside, are 1 in. high, ½ in. thick, and 3½ in. long.

The chairs are fastened by spikes to wooden sleepers 4 ft long, 6 in. wide, and 3 in. thick; these lie from 2 to 3 ft apart, and the gauge of the rails is 32 in. Inside the rails the track is carefully covered with gravel, above which the rails project ¾ in. The haulage is by horses.

A Prussian foot of such rail weighs somewhat over 6 lb, therefore a running fathom (13⅓ ft) weighs 81½ lb. A cast-iron chair of this kind weighs 4⅓ lb; there are six chairs to the fathom, totalling 26 lb. Therefore, according to the prices in the Liverpool & Manchester Railway estimates, one running fathom costs:—

In rails	3 thl. 14 grs. 6 pfg.
In chairs	1 thl. 1 grs. 7 pfg.
Together	4 thl. 16 grs. 1 pfg.

[1] *The German text is 'Englische Schienenwege (Railroads)'.—Ed.*

VII. Wrought-Iron Railway at the Consolidated Mines

At the large copper mines, called the Consolidated Mines, near Redruth, in Cornwall, 160 fathoms (of 6 ft Engl.) or $139\frac{3}{4}$ fathoms Pruss. below the surface, and 120 fathoms ($104\frac{4}{5}$ fathoms Pruss.) below the gallery bottom, in the deep sump stretch of Taylor shaft, there is a railway of similar construction to that just described. It consists of wrought-iron rails $2\frac{1}{4}$ in. high, $\frac{3}{4}$ in. wide, and 12 ft and more long. These rails also are fixed by wedges in cast-iron chairs, which are spiked to longitudinal wooden planks 8 in. wide and 2 in. thick, and require as much running length as the wooden sleepers of the preceding railway; on the other hand, the two rails are not connected with one another, and can easily get out of gauge alignment. Nevertheless, this method can be advantageous with continuous horse haulage, as the gravel lying on cross-sleepers is very hurtful to the horses, and the sleepers easily may be worn through. The iron chairs are 35 in. from centre to centre. The rails are somewhat more convex on the upper face than the former, and fully rounded, so that they have no level surface at the top. There is a groove rolled in them, on one side only, for driving in the wedge, and this appears to be sufficient. These rails are lighter than the preceding; 1 ft Pruss. weighs somewhat over $5\frac{1}{2}$ lb, so that 1 running fathom weighs $74\frac{1}{2}$ lb. The chairs, on the other hand, are heavier and weigh 6 lb each. A running fathom requires $4\frac{1}{2}$ chairs, the weight of which amounts to just as much as on the preceding railway. The cost of a running fathom is

For rails	3 thl. 5 grs. 6 pfg.
In chairs	1 thl. 2 grs. 8 pfg.
Together	4 thl. 8 grs. 2 pfg.

The gauge of the rails is 20 in. The wagons which run on this line are made of iron plate; they weigh 3 cwt when empty, and hold $3\frac{1}{2}$ Kübel, or 16 cwt of ore. They are moved by a wagon pusher. These wagons are provided with a door at one end, which hangs on a crossbar at the top and is locked at the bottom by a bolt. Thc iron body rests on two strong cross-timbers, to which the wrought-iron axles, as well as the iron body, arc fastened by three bolts. The wheels are 12 in. high and 2 in. wide; they are of cast-iron with two flanges, in order, as the Steiger (Captain) said, that they might follow the track more easily on the curves. The naves are 3 in. long, the axles are 1 to $1\frac{1}{8}$ in. diameter; each flange is $\frac{1}{2}$ in. thick. The wheels have four spokes. The wheel centres are 19 in. apart. The wagon body holds about 7·8 cu. ft.

VIII. Wrought-Iron Railway at the Harriot Shaft of the Dolcoath Mine

At the Harriot shaft of the Dolcoath Mine, near Redruth in Cornwall, there is a wrought-iron railway with a tipping wagon for the despatch of ore and rock. The wrought-iron rail is $12\frac{1}{2}$ ft long, $\frac{2}{3}$ in. thick, and $1\frac{3}{4}$ in. high, and at each end there are welded-on ears $1\frac{3}{4}$ in. wide, $\frac{1}{2}$ in. thick, and 2 in. long, by means of which the rails are spiked to the wooden sleepers. Sleepers of wrought-iron are also used, which serve the purpose of giving the rails more rigidity between the fastening points. The rails lie partly on longitudinal timbers and partly on simple wooden sleepers. One Prussian foot of this rail weighs 4 lb, therefore a running fathom (of $13\frac{1}{3}$ ft) weighs $53\frac{1}{3}$ lb. On a fathom, however, two fixing sleepers are necessary, which weigh 12 lb, so that a running fathom of this railway requires $65\frac{1}{3}$ lb of wrought-iron; at the above-mentioned price this costs 2 thl. 23 grs. 4 pfg. The line has a gauge of $34\frac{1}{2}$ in. The tipping wagon is of iron plate, holding 14 cu. ft, and turns about one axle. The wheels are 12 in. high, $1\frac{1}{2}$ in. wide, and have only one flange, which is not on the inner side of the rail as is usual on all other English railways, but on the outer side. The nave is 4 in. long and the axle 1 in. thick. The flange projects $1\frac{1}{4}$ in. and is $\frac{1}{2}$ in. thick. There are four spokes in the wheel. The wheel centres are 15 in. apart. On the wagon body there is a pair of claw clamps by means of which the body catches upon the rails during tipping and so cannot overturn.

IX. Wrought-Iron Railway at the New Whim Shaft of the Dolcoath Mine

In the 70 fathom (of 6 ft Engl., 61 fathoms Pruss.) gallery of the New Whim shaft of the same mine, there is a wrought-iron railway of similar construction, upon which runs a haulage wagon of iron plate. The rails are $\frac{2}{3}$ to $\frac{5}{6}$ in. thick and $1\frac{1}{2}$ to 2 in. high, provided at the ends with welded-on ears 2 in. long and $1\frac{1}{2}$ in. wide. The sleepers on which they rest are 6 in. wide and $2\frac{1}{2}$ in. thick. The gauge is only $9\frac{1}{2}$ to $9\frac{5}{6}$ in. The wagon contains $5\frac{1}{3}$ cu.ft. The axles, of $1\frac{1}{4}$ in. diameter, lie in iron hoops in which they can turn. The wheels are 3 in. wide, 12 in. high, and have two flanges, each of which is $\frac{1}{4}$ in. thick and projects $\frac{1}{2}$ in.; the naves are $3\frac{1}{4}$ in. long. One Prussian foot of this rail weighs 3·4 to 5·6 lb and therefore a running fathom weighs $45\frac{1}{3}$ to $73\frac{1}{2}$ lb.

X. Wrought-Iron Railway at the Shaft and Stamping Mill of the East Crinnis Mine near St Austle

At the East Crinnis Mine, near St Austle, in Cornwall, a wrought-iron railway runs from the shaft to the stamping mill and serves to transport the ore to be crushed.

The rails are 2 in. high and $\frac{1}{2}$ in. wide, and are fixed in cast-iron chairs by wedges, in the same manner as on the wrought-iron railways previously described, in that a small groove is rolled on one side of the rail. One Prussian foot of this rail weighs $3\frac{3}{8}$ lb, and therefore a running fathom weighs 45 lb. According to the price already mentioned, this costs 1 thl. 27 grs. 8 pfg. The chairs at the mine are partly forged and partly cast; they are fastened by four spikes to wooden sleepers or longitudinal timbers.

At the sidings cast-iron point and crossing pieces are provided. These are 2 ft to 2 ft 8 in. long, $4\frac{1}{2}$ to 7 in. wide, and are so arranged that the rails can be joined to the ends. Where one track separates from the other, there is a movable tongue by which one or other track of the railway can be opened or closed. The wagons used on this railway are of iron plate and are arranged for tipping; they are moved by two men and contain $3\frac{1}{2}$ cu. ft. and about 25 cwt of ore. The wheels are 15 in. high, have one flange on the inner side, and are 2 in. wide; the axles are 1 in. diameter and their centres are 18 in. from one another. There is a dust cover on the wagon above the wheels, which is very helpful but is not often used. The gauge is 26 in.

As the railway slopes more steeply than is either necessary or advantageous for the haulage, with more favourable conditions of country, a larger load could probably be moved.

A similar railway links the scattered buildings of the Carclaze tin mine near St Austle. The rails are quite smooth, 3 in. high, $\frac{2}{3}$ in. thick, and 15 ft long. The chairs also are of wrought-iron; they consist of a plate 6 in. long and $2\frac{1}{2}$ in. wide on which two side-walls $1\frac{1}{2}$ in. high are rivetted. These chairs are spiked to wooden sleepers placed 3 ft apart. The gauge of the line is 23 in. The wagon is arranged very conveniently for tipping. The body contains nearly 14 cu. ft. The wagon consists of a small frame 2 ft long, and $1\frac{1}{2}$ ft wide, on which the axles are fixed. Upon this frame lies a platform, which is able to turn about a strong upright bolt, so that the body, which is fastened to the platform by two hinges, may be tipped to either side. The wheels are $12\frac{1}{2}$ in. high and $2\frac{1}{2}$ in. wide. The flange projects $1\frac{1}{6}$ in.; it is $\frac{1}{4}$ in. thick at the edge and 1 in. thick at the wheel rim. The nave is $5\frac{1}{4}$ in. long and very conical. The axle on a length of 8 in., decreases from $1\frac{3}{4}$ in. to $1\frac{1}{12}$ in. These wagons, filled with tin ore, can hold 16–18 cwt, and are moved by one man.

C. GERMAN RAILWAYS (TRAMROADS)[1]

The German railway, which has a flange on the rails and no flange on the wheel, is very often employed in England, especially in the Southern and Midland counties. In South Wales, where there are very many railways, they are nearly all of this kind. But here also, for larger schemes, they

[1] *The German text is 'Deutsche Schienenwege (Tramroads)'.—Ed.*

are now convinced of the advantages of the English railways,[1] which were first perfected in the North of England, and especially at Newcastle. Where in a region there are already many railways of one kind, it is difficult to introduce new ones of another sort, as the advantage of connecting them would thereby be lost. These tramroads are formed only of cast-iron, and none of the kind is made of wrought-iron.

XI. Tramroad from Portreath to the Mines near Redruth

From Portreath, a small harbour on the north coast of Cornwall, a tramroad 5 miles Engl. long is laid to different mines in the neighbourhood of Redruth, and is used principally for the transport of copper ore and coal.[2] It consists of cast-iron rails 3 ft Engl. long, and has a gauge of about 44 in. Engl. Wooden wagons with cast-iron wheels run on this. The wagons hold about 3 tons (60 cwt) of ore, which is drawn by one horse.

The rails are 3 in. wide, exclusive of the flange; the flange is $1\frac{3}{4}$ in. high, $\frac{5}{8}$ in. thick at the top, and $1\frac{1}{4}$ in. at the bottom. The rail is $\frac{7}{8}$ in. thick, and underneath has a reinforcement $1\frac{1}{4}$ in. wide and $\frac{1}{8}$ in. thick. Small buttresses are provided at the ends on the inner side, with a notch in the middle by which the rails are fixed to the stone sleepers; the latter are 8 in. square. A wooden plug is driven into a hole bored in the stone, and in this a spike is driven, the head of which is sunk into both rails where they butt together. On the crossing piece, where two rails intersect, flanges are provided on both sides. Where one rail diverges from another, the flange is formed of a movable tongue.

The wagon bodies, which have a content of 55 cu. ft, consist of a framework of 3-in. timber covered inside with 1 in. boards. The axles lie in cast-iron bearings screwed to the wagon body, and the wheels turn on the axles. The wheels are 24 in. high and are only $\frac{3}{4}$ in. wide at the circumference. They have six spokes, each of which divides into two arms towards the rim. The naves are 6 in. long and the axles are $1\frac{1}{2}$ in. diameter.

XII. Cast-Iron Tramroad at the Landore Colliery near Swansea

At Landore Colliery on the Tawe Canal[3] 2 miles north of Swansea, where the mine tramway reaches a length of 1,700 yards (5,100 ft Engl.) 743 fathoms Pruss., there is a cast-iron tramroad with a gauge of 27 in. The rails are 3 ft 10 in. long, $\frac{5}{8}$ in. thick, and, without the flange, 3 in. wide; the flange is $1\frac{3}{4}$ in. high; $\frac{1}{4}$ in. wide at the top, and $\frac{1}{2}$ in. wide at the bottom. These rails are fixed into one another in a not unsuitable manner. At one end of each rail there is a circular addition which projects $1\frac{1}{8}$ in., and in which there is a conical hole the larger diameter of which is $2\frac{1}{4}$ in. On the other end of each rail there is a conical piece on the underside which fits into the hole in the next following rail.

Through these pieces there is a hole, through which a wooden peg is driven in order to fasten both rails to the wooden sleeper; the latter are about 5 in. wide, 2 in. thick, and 40 in. long. Fifty pieces of this rail, together about 192 ft long, weigh about 1 ton, and for the ton £7 (49 thl.) is paid. One cwt of rails costs 2 thl. 13 grs. 6 pfg. One Prussian fathom of these rails weighs, therefore, 152 lb and costs 3 thl. 11 grs. 6 pfg.

---

[1] *The German text refers to 'Englische Schienenwege (Railroads)'.—Ed.*

[2] *This tramroad was built by Messrs Foxes, merchants of Falmouth, who were lessees of Lord de Dunstanville (Francis Basset). The first rail was laid by Lord de Dunstanville 'under a salute of cannon at Portreath batteries' on Wednesday* 25 *October* 1809, *on the occasion of a national jubilee marking the* 49*th anniversary of the accession of King George III. The precise date of opening of the line has not been traced. It extended from Portreath Harbour to various mines at Scorrier and Poldice. The tramroad was used extensively until about* 1864, *and was not dismantled until the end of the nineteenth century.—Ed.*

[3] *The Swansea Canal, running parallel with the River Tawe. It was incorporated by Act of* 23 *May* 1794 (34 *Geo. III, cap.* 109). *The engineer was Thomas Sheasby. In the 'Cyclopaedia' by Dr Abraham Rees it is stated that the canal was completed in October* 1798. *Some sections were in use earlier.—Ed.*

Horses perform the haulage on this tramroad. The coal wagons are 2 ft high, 6 ft long, and 2 ft 3 in. wide, in the clear, and therefore contain 27 cu. ft. The contents of $12\frac{1}{2}$ such wagons are 1 Way = 216 Winchester bushels of coal. One bushel of coal is $\frac{3}{4}$ cwt; therefore a Way, or nine loads, would be 162 cwt. The weight of a Way, however, is given as 200 cwt, or 10 tons, which may be due partly to overloading; and one horse, therefore, draws somewhat less than one ton (*sic*) of coal. The wagons show nothing note-worthy in their construction. The wheels are of cast-iron and are 14 in. diameter. They are very narrow and therefore cut into the rails very easily; at the circumference, the width is only $\frac{1}{4}$ in. The nave is $3\frac{1}{2}$ in. long. The wheels are cast as discs $\frac{1}{2}$ in. thick, without real spokes, but have in them four circular holes of $2\frac{3}{4}$ in. diameter. It is not necessary to enlarge about the weight of these.

At Landore the daily output is about 20 Way = 200 tons, or 4,000 cwt of coal, for which 10 horses in the mine and about 50 workmen, namely 20 hewers and 30 helpers, are necessary. The 30 helpers bring the coal out of the side galleries into the main hauling gallery, and use smaller wagons, twelve of which are required to fill one larger horse wagon.

Fourteen English miles north of Swansea up the canal lies the Cwrnllyn Fell Colliery. A tramroad 3 miles long, which is not very well maintained, leads from the canal to the colliery. On this run wagons holding somewhat more than 1 ton, and two of these are drawn by one horse. The wheels of these wagons are of cast-iron 18 in. high, provided with 12 spokes. The naves are $6\frac{1}{4}$ in. long. These wheels are exceptionally narrow, only $\frac{1}{8}$ in. wide at the circumference, but this is usual on the tramroads of this district. They are movable on the axles, while the axles, which are of wrought-iron, also turn in their bearings.

XIII. Cast-Iron Tramroad from Swansea to Oystermouth

The bay of Swansea is too shallow at ebb-tide to permit vessels to enter Swansea harbour, and they are accustomed to anchor off Oystermouth, a small fishing village 5 miles Engl. from Swansea.

Also, there are extensive limestone quarries close to Oystermouth which supply hewn-stone and mortar, so that generally there is a large and vigorous traffic between Swansea and Oystermouth. In order to facilitate and increase this traffic, a tramroad has been laid between these two places. It is about 7 miles Engl. long and has a gauge of 47 in.[1] The track follows the coast and is entirely level. The rails are 35 in. long,[1] $3\frac{1}{2}$ in. wide, without the flange; $\frac{1}{2}$ in. thick, except at the ends, where they are $\frac{5}{8}$ in. thick. The flange is $2\frac{1}{2}$ in. high, $\frac{1}{3}$ in. thick at the top, and $\frac{1}{2}$ in. at the bottom. The fastening upon stone sleepers is the same as on the Portreath Tramroad.

The line, also, is specially intended for the quick transport of travellers; in the summer months a kind of coach runs on it, in which about 20 passengers are drawn by one horse. This tramroad does not present any peculiarities.

XIV. Tramroads in the Region of Merthyr Tydwill[2]

In the neighbourhood of Merthyr Tydwill, where there are many blast-furnaces, there is a considerable number of tramroads for leading coal, coke, ironstone, and limestone to the furnaces,

[1] *It will be noticed that, in this paragraph, the dimensions are not given in both English and Prussian measurements. The rails (some of which have survived) are known to have been* 3 *English ft long. E. A. Forward commented that, as the length of the rails is given as* 35 *in., the authors were evidently using Prussian measures in which* 3 *English ft equal* 34·96 *Prussian in. He assumed, therefore, that the gauge of* 47 *Prussian in.* (48·4 *English in.*) *was intended to indicate* 4 *English ft between the flanges of the rails.*

The Oystermouth Railway or Tramroad Company was incorporated by Act of Parliament on 29 *June* 1804 (44 *Geo. III, cap.* 55). *The first cash-receipts book does not seem to have survived, but a limited goods traffic was conveyed as early as April* 1806. *Passenger traffic, by a contractor, began on* 25 *March* 1807, *the earliest known date of the regular conveyance of passengers by rail.—Ed.*

[2] *In English, usually spelled Merthyr Tydfil.—Ed.*

both over and underground. These are all constructed in a similar manner, but are by no means distinguished by their fitness or good maintenance. They are often led uphill and downhill on far from the most advantageous angles of slope, and are frequently in a very dilapidated condition. Horses are used almost universally for haulage. One horse usually draws not more than 2 tons. Self-acting planes or other ingenious arrangements are not evident.

These tramroads were first planned in 1791, and in 1811 they already amounted to 150 miles Engl. (31½ miles Pruss.) above ground alone. The first to be laid out by the authority of an Act of Parliament (1794) lies on the Cardiff or Glamorganshire Canal, the upper part of which often suffers from lack of water; it is specially useful to the iron furnaces of Merthyr Tydwill. The length of this is 26¾ miles Engl. (5⅔ miles Pruss.).[1]

One such cast-iron tramroad lies at the Bute Ironworks, 4 miles from Merthyr Tydwill. The rails are 44 in. long, 3 in. wide without the flange, and ¾ in. thick; the flange is 2½ in. high, ¼ in. thick at the top, and 1 in. at the bottom. The notch at each end for fastening is like that used on the rails of the Portreath Tramroad. The gauge is 32 in. The rails rest on cast-iron sleepers, upon which they fit into a slot 4¼ in. wide and 1 in. deep, and are there fixed by spikes. Such cast-iron sleepers are often employed here, where pig-iron is very cheap. Other similar sleepers on a tramroad near the Pen-y-daran Ironworks are entirely flat on top, and the rails are fixed to them by wooden pegs only. On the Bute Tramroad there is a wagon which is composed of iron bars, in addition to the ordinary wooden wagons. The wheels are of cast-iron, and are very narrow, as on all the tramroads in this region. In consequence, they affect the rails injuriously. The wheels are 19¾ in. in diameter; the rim is 1 in. thick and rounded; the nave is 6 in. long. The axles are 2 in. in diameter; they rest in turned axle seats so that they can rotate in these seats, and the wheels also turn on the axles.

Many other similar tramroads are in use, of which only the following brief account is possible.

The Aberdare Canal, which forms a branch of the Cardiff Canal, is connected with the Neath Canal, by a tramroad; a very large inclined plane with a high-pressure engine accomplishes this connection.

The Sirhoway Tramroad begins by the Monmouthshire Canal at Pillgwelly, goes through Tredegar Park up the Ebbw River; crosses that river at Risca on a bridge with 16 arches; and leads past the Tredegar and Sirhoway Ironworks to the Trevill limestone quarries. The whole length amounts to 28 miles Engl. (5⅞ miles Pruss.). From this tramroad branches go to different collieries, one to the Rumney Ironworks, and two to the Monmouthshire Canal. On this line one horse will draw downwards 10 tons, 200 cwt, and bring upwards the empty wagons, a performance which far surpasses that usual on the tramroads of South Wales.

The Brinore Tramroad leads from the Sirhoway line over the Black Mountain to the Vale of the Usk at Brecon, and thence to Hay on the Wye. Through these connections, the price of coal in the upper parts of the counties of Hereford and Radnor is very low.

The Blaen Avon Tramroad leads from the Monmouthshire Canal to the Blaen Avon Ironworks, a length of 5½ miles Engl., and rises 610 ft in that distance.

The Caermarthenshire Tramroad begins at the shipwharves and harbour at Llanelly and extends a distance of 15 miles through a very productive coalfield to the limestone quarry near Llandebie;

[1] *The authors give no details of this line, and their brief reference is based presumably on verbal information, which they misinterpreted, of an intention which was never carried out in its entirety. The alleged Act of Parliament of* 1794 *cannot be traced, and there is no evidence that the canal was ever paralleled by a tramroad excepting for the* 9½ *miles from Merthyr to Abercynon, by the partners of three ironworks under an agreement of* 18 *January* 1799. *This was the famous Penydarren Tramroad, opened in* 1802 *as a* 4 *ft* 2 *in. plateway, the line on which Trevithick ran a locomotive in* 1804.—*Ed.*

many branches on the east side lead to important collieries. The chief transport thereon consists of coal, iron, and limestone. The line was planned in 1801.[1]

The Abergavenny Tramroad begins at the Brecknock Canal and leads by means of a bridge over the Usk to Abergavenny. Tramroads from the same canal lead to the Usk and to Hay, and several others to coal mines and ironworks. At the ironworks near Pontypool there are some very high inclined planes.

The Ruabon Brook Tramroad goes from an extensive basin at Pontcysylte, on the north bank of the River Dee. It is a double line, and leads by a gentle ascent past the Hazledine Ironworks to Ruabon Brook, a distance of 3 miles Engl.

XV. Surrey Tramroad

Among similar tramroads, the Surrey Tramroad, near London, is especially interesting. It begins on the south side of the Thames at Wandsworth, in Surrey, and proceeds for a distance of 9½ miles Engl. in a south-easterly direction to Croydon; thence it goes south for 8½ miles Engl. to Merstham. The total length is 18 miles Engl. or 3¾ miles Pruss. The Acts of Parliament which sanctioned this plan were passed between 1800 and 1804.[2] It has a double track; the gradient is at no point more severe than $\frac{1}{120}$, or 28⅗ min. of angle. The first rails employed were 4 in. wide on the flat and nearly 1 in. thick, with a flange 3 in. high and ½ in. thick. These have become much damaged by the use of narrow wheel treads, as deep grooves are made. At present, therefore, rails are used with a strengthening rib underneath which is highest in the middle and tapers to nothing at the ends; so also are the upper flanges made higher at the middle than at the ends, to give more strength to the rails.

The wagons which run on this line weigh about 1 ton; they are 5 ft wide, 8 ft long, and 2 ft deep, and have a capacity, therefore of 80 cu. ft. Engl. They do not exceed 65 cwt when laden, but the usual load is 60 cwt. The cast-iron wheels are 32 in. in diameter and are 1½ in. wide at the tread. The axles are conical, from 2⅜ in. to 1½ in. diameter.

The line is intended for general traffic; it has, however, not completely achieved its objective and has anything but encouraged similar undertakings. This arises partly because the performance of wagons on tramroads is not nearly so favourable as it is upon English railways (*Railroads*); the wagons are heavy and inconvenient for the transport of goods in large pieces. As the wagons are confined to the tramroad, the goods must be distributed to their final destination points by other means. Therefore, short tramroads for general use seldom achieve their objective.

Similar tramroads, but with special aims, are as follow:—

Dewsbury and Birstal Tramroad,[3] from the colliery to the Calder and Hebble Canal, a length of 3 miles Engl.; completed in 1805.

The Ashby-de-la-Zouch Canal is fed by many tramroads: one of 3⅜ miles Engl. to the Ticknall

[1] *The Carmarthenshire Railway or Tramroad Company was incorporated on* 3 *June* 1802 *by Act of* 42 *Geo. III, cap.* 80, *under the authority of which this tramroad was built. According to the 'Cyclopaedia' by Abraham Rees, the line (which involved substantial embankment) was completed in November* 1804.—*Ed.*

[2] *The Act of Parliament incorporating the Surrey Iron Railway Company* (41 *Geo. III, cap.* 33) *received the Royal Assent on* 21 *May* 1801. *It authorised the line from Wandsworth to Croydon. The Croydon, Merstham & Godstone Iron Railway Company was incorporated by Act of* 17 *May* 1803 (43 *Geo. III, cap.* 35). *Although authorised to extend from Croydon to Godstone and to Reigate, it was not built beyond Merstham (which the German authors spell Mertsham). The S.I.R. obtained further Acts in* 1805 *and* 1806; *the C.M. & G.I.R. in* 1806. *The line was opened from Wandsworth to Croydon on* 26 *July* 1803; *and from Croydon to Merstham on* 24 *July* 1805. *There are some indications, however, that a limited traffic was carried before the 'openings'.*—*Ed.*

[3] *Dr Abraham Rees, in his 'Cyclopaedia', states that this line extended from the Calder and Hebble Navigation at Dewsbury to the Stubley coal mines, worked by Thomas Chester & Sons, the sole proprietors of this railway, which was completed in October* 1805.—*Ed.*

limestone quarries; one of 5 miles Engl. to the Measham Colliery; and one of 6½ miles Engl. to the Cloud Hill limestone quarries.

The Derby Canal has several tramroads to Horseley Colliery; to Smithy Houses 4 miles Engl. long; to Smalley Mills 1½ miles Engl. long. So also the Cromford and Erewash Canal is connected with many tramroads. The Charnwood Forest Canal is connected with the Soar Navigation by a tramroad 2½ miles Engl. long and with a rise of 185 ft.

From the Peak Forest Canal, near Chapel Milton, a tramroad 6 miles Engl. long runs to the Loads Knowl limestone quarry, with an inclined plane 1,545 ft long and a fall of 204 ft, a slope of $\frac{1}{7\cdot 5}$.

The Lancaster Canal Tramroad runs from Clayton Green across the Ribble valley, a distance of 3¼ miles Engl., to the opposite slope; this connects the parts of the canal and has inclined planes on each of the two valley slopes.

From the River Wye, near Mitchell Dean, a tramroad through the Forest of Dean to Lydney on the Severn, with a branch past Coleford to Monmouth; another tramroad 5 miles Engl. long leads from the Severn to the collieries of the Forest of Dean.

At the many collieries and ironworks in Staffordshire, in the neighbourhood of Dudley, and in the large limestone quarries of the district, only one kind of railway is employed—German cast-iron rails, *Tramroads*—which also rest on cast-iron sleepers. The cast-iron sleepers are 2 in. thick, 3 to 4 in. wide, and at each end have a 9-in. long and wide extension upon which is a dovetail-shaped notch, in which the rails can be fixed easily. At each end, outside the flange, the rails have a part becoming wider at the bottom, which fits into the notch in the sleeper. The rails are often only ½ in. thick, and 2¼ in. wide; the flange is likewise ½ in. thick and is 1½ in. high. On curves, cast curved rails are used. These are provided with a very strong flange from 1 in. to 1¼ in. thick, because it is affected more injuriously than on the straight parts of the line. Where the tramroad crosses other public roads or highways, stronger rails provided with two flanges are used. They form a narrow channel into which the wheels of passing road vehicles cannot slip. The upper surface of these two edges is better made uneven, by small arc-shaped projections, than cast wholly smooth, so that wheels travelling across the rail shall not slip to and fro. This kind of rail is used not only here but wherever tramroads cross public roads.

Hereabouts, in Coalbrookdale, a cast-iron tramroad runs from the Severn to the lower iron smelting works of the Dale Company. As is the case with all tramroads in this district, it belongs to the same species. The rails are 5 and even 5½ ft long, and lie in cast-iron sleepers. The tramroads at Coalbrookdale are of two sizes. The smaller one is of 20 in. gauge, and the haulage on this is performed with small trucks; it lies in the middle of a larger line of 36 in. gauge. Horse haulage is used thereon. It, perhaps, merits remark that the smallest gauge for horse use employed anywhere is to be found in this district, as on some lines the gauge is only 18 in.

At the Horshay Ironworks, which also belongs to the Dale Company, there are tipping wagons with sheet-iron bodies on wooden frames, very suitable for the transport of blast-furnace slag. The wheels on these wagons are from 14 to 18 in. diameter, and have wider wheel rims than are employed elsewhere in England, and especially in South Wales, namely 1¼ to 1½ in.

All these rails are so laid that the flange lies on the inner side, and at the same time holds together the hauling path.

XVI. Self-acting Plane in the Limestone Quarry to the Avon Canal near Bath

In connection with the cast-iron tramroads previously mentioned, no self-acting and inclined planes are described. The provision of alternate horizontal, or nearly horizontal, stretches of line, and of inclined planes by means of which difficulties of terrain are overcome, was first accomplished with the laying out of well-constructed English railways (*Railroads*). Nevertheless, to link stone quarries, canals, and sloping shafts with longer railways, several inclined planes and self-acting planes have been made with the tramroad kind of rail.

From the large limestone quarry near Bath, which supplied much hewn stone, there is a self-acting plane with a length of 2,658 ft Engl. (387 fathoms Pruss.) to the Avon Canal upon which the stone is conveyed further. This self-acting plane has two divisions. The upper division, 1,658 ft long, is not of uniform slope; it is very little at the top, up to 10 degrees in the middle, and at the bottom is both inclined and curved. The lower division has a uniform inclination of about 5 degrees. The total perpendicular height of the self-acting plane is 480 to 500 ft. The whole length is traversed by a double cast-iron German tramroad. Crossing switches are provided, serving both lines at the quarry, for each of the brake arrangements, and below at the canal. Each track has a gauge of 3 ft 4 in., and they lie the same distance from one another.

The separate rails are $2\frac{1}{2}$ ft long, $3\frac{1}{2}$ in. wide, and $\frac{5}{8}$ in. thick. The flange is $2\frac{1}{2}$ in. high, $\frac{7}{12}$ in. wide at the bottom, and $\frac{3}{3}$ (*sic*) in. high at the top. On the underside, close to the outer edge, is an arc-shaped strengthening rib 1 in. high in the middle and tapering to nothing. The ends of the rails are $\frac{3}{4}$ in. thick and are provided with a small addition at the inner side; they have a notch whereby the rails, two and two together, are fixed by an iron spike with a square pyramidal head. The rails rest on stone sleepers and the spikes are driven into wooden plugs therein. These rails are too weak for the load which is lowered on them, and which amounts to 80 cwt including the wagon. This is proved by the large heaps of broken rails that lie beside the line; nevertheless, the newly-delivered rails are cast no stronger.

At the upper part of the line there is a conical rope drum on a horizontal axle, which is provided, on one side, with a horizontal brake wheel; the drum is 5 ft diameter at the ends and 6 ft in the middle, and is 11 ft long. The rope by which the wagons on this part of the line are lowered is $1\frac{1}{4}$ in. diameter and untarred; it runs over wooden friction rollers 34 in. long, 6 in. diameter, with iron pivots. The iron sockets in which these pivots turn are let into the stone sleepers on which the rails rest. As the rope drum is longer than the width of the railway, the highest friction roller is provided with flanges, and so arranged that it can slip to and fro on its axle.

On the lower part of the line, the brake arrangement consists of a rope sheave lying at the level of the rails on an upright shaft with a tilt of 6 in. This sheave is of cast-iron 8in. high, has a projecting rim on the outer side, and is 6 ft 8 in. diameter, so that the chain whereon the wagons are lowered lies directly in the middle of the track. This chain has straight links $4\frac{1}{4}$ in. long, $2\frac{1}{4}$ in. wide, and is made of $\frac{5}{8}$ in. round iron. The brake wheels is on the same axle, under the rope sheave. It has a diameter of 9 ft, and a height of 8 in., and is surrounded for $\frac{3}{4}$ of the circumference by jointed wooden brake-checks which can be drawn tight by a single fork connection.

This chain runs over cast-iron friction sheaves, erected 24 ft apart on separate stone sleepers in the middle of the track. These are 9 in. diameter, are $7\frac{1}{2}$ in. long, have $1\frac{1}{2}$ in. rims, and are fast keyed on wrought-iron axles 15 in. long, which run in small cast-iron bearings.

The wagons, on which up to 70 cwt of stone is loaded, consist of a wooden platform provided with an iron railing $2\frac{1}{2}$ ft high. The platform is composed of four frame-beams $7\frac{1}{2}$ ft long, 7 in. high, and 5 in. thick, bound together by four cross-beams and some iron cramps. The axles are of cast-iron $3\frac{1}{2}$ in. high and $3\frac{1}{4}$ in. wide. The round part of the axle in the nave of the wheel is $9\frac{1}{4}$ in. long, $1\frac{1}{2}$ in. diameter in front, and $2\frac{1}{2}$ in. behind. These axles are let 2 in. deep into the cross-beams, which are 8 in. square. The axle-centres are 40 in. apart. The wheels are $16\frac{1}{2}$ in. high, 1 in. thick at the rim, with 6 spoke-like ribs between which holes are made. The length of the nave is $7\frac{3}{4}$ in. One such wagon, with its wheels, weighs 10 cwt. The narrow wheels probably contribute greatly to the number of broken rails. Here, where any increased friction arising from wider wheels could not be disadvantageous, they have no advantage whatever.

XVII. Self-acting Plane and Tramroad from the Granite Quarry near Dalkey to Kingstown, near Dublin

The granite quarry to Dalkey, 7 miles Engl. from Dublin, supplies excellent large hewn stone, which serves for various purposes and was often employed for building the harbour at Kingstown. Thence leads a 2-mile Engl. tramroad.[1] In the neighbourhood of the quarry, this has three self-acting planes, with inclinations of about 10 degrees, and of which the lowest and longest is about 100 fathoms Pruss. long.

On the self-acting planes, there are two tracks 3 ft apart, and each of 4 ft gauge. The rails are similar to those on the previously described self-acting plane,[2] only more durably and strongly constructed. Each rail is 3 ft long, 4 in. wide, including the flange, and 1 in. thick. The flange is 2 in. high, $\frac{3}{4}$ in. at the top, and 1 in. wide at the bottom. On the underside of the rail there are two strengthening ribs $\frac{3}{4}$ in. wide and projecting $\frac{1}{2}$ in. The ends of the rails are made $1\frac{1}{2}$ in. thick for a length of 4 in., and provided with small buttresses. They are fastened directly upon granite blocks, as were the rails previously mentioned. The brake arrangements on the three inclined planes are alike. An endless chain passes round a cast-iron pulley lying at the level of the rail at the top of the self-acting plane, and round two small guide sheaves at the bottom; a brake wheel is fixed to the top pulley. In front of each of these pulleys is a vertical hanging roller, whereby the chain is guided to it. The upper pulley is cast in one piece with the brake wheel, is 7 ft diameter and 15 in. high, and is provided with a groove for the chain and also with flanges. The arms and centre piece are cast separately, and screwed to the inside of the pulley. The axle of this pulley is 8 ft long and is considerably thicker at the top than at the bottom. The brake consists of an iron band 5 in. wide, and surrounding only half the wheel; it can, however, be pressed very tightly against the wheel by a double lever connection. The lower guiding sheaves also lie at the level of, and parallel with the lines, and are mounted on iron axles. The full wagons to be braked downwards, and the empty wagons to be drawn upwards, are fastened to the endless chain by a chain provided with a strong hook. This chain is attached to the lower end of the wagon, so that, at the top, it goes away under the wagon, which attachment is specially advantageous, and in other respects, at least, has no disadvantage. In this manner two or three full wagons are separately attached to the chain, with just as many empty ones on the other side, so that the upward-hauling and downward-letting continue steadily.

The wagons consist of a strong platform, which, for the transport of the larger stones, are without bodies. For the smaller stones they have a body with a door at each end which is hinged at the bottom and fixed at the top by eyes and linchpins. At each end there are two hooks on both frame-beams, on which the chains are hooked. The wagons are 4 ft wide and 6 ft long; the axle centres are 3 ft apart.

The axles are of wrought-iron, and are fastened to the wagon by three screws. They are 3 in. wide, $4\frac{1}{2}$ in. high, and are entirely let into the cross-beams. The cast-iron wheels are 18 in. high, have a rim $1\frac{1}{2}$ in. wide, and six spoke-like projections with circular holes between them. The nave is 6 in. long where it surrounds the axle, and is provided with a 4 in. extension which encloses the linchpin and prevents it from jumping out, a contrivance which is copied from the ordinary wheels of the freight wagons in England, and seems to be very suitable for the purpose. A notch allows the linchpin to be inserted.

[1] *The line was built about* 1816 *by the Commissioners appointed for the erection of Dunleary Harbour, to facilitate the conveyance of granite from the Dalkey quarries to the harbour site. The visit of King George IV in* 1821 *resulted in a change of name to Kingstown, and the harbour was well-known as such until* 1920, *when it reverted to the earlier name, but in the Irish form of Dun Laoghaire. In the later years, one of two tracks of this railway was taken over on* 26 *September* 1842 *for use as a public atmospheric railway extension of the Dublin & Kingstown Railway. As such it was used from* 3 *October* 1843 *until* 12 *April* 1854.—*Ed.*

[2] *Presumably meaning that near Bath.—Ed.*

XVIII. Diagonal inclined adit at the Wheal-Friendship Mine near Mary Tavy, close by Tavistock

At the Wheal-Friendship mine, near Mary Tavy outside Tavistock, in Devonshire, there is an inclined plane or adit on the line of the copper load, which reaches from the surface down to the 112 fathom (98 fathoms Pruss.) bottom, and is arranged for ore hauling. The length of this gallery is estimated to be 450 fathoms (2,700 ft Engl.)[1], 393 fathoms Pruss., and, although this estimate is perhaps too high, the length nevertheless is very considerable; the line extends about 20 fathoms on the surface. A length of 450 fathoms and a vertical depth of 112 fathoms (672 ft) gives a mean angle of descent of 14½ degrees. The fall of the gallery is not uniform and amounts to more than 14½ degrees at many points; also, the gallery follows the inequalities of the lode, and therefore has frequent curves. Side galleries are driven out of this gallery at vertical distances of 10 fathoms, and, for the deeper workings, side shafts are brought from the lode to reach the main hauling gallery.

In this inclined adit is a single cast-iron German tramroad of 36 in. gauge. The cast-iron rails are mostly 6 ft long and 3 in. wide without the flange; the latter is 2 in. high, ½ in. thick at the bottom, and ⅜ in. thick at the top; the base of the rail is ¾ in. thick. Shorter pieces of 3 ft long and less are used at crossings. The rails have a square hole at each end and are fastened by iron spokes to wooden sleepers; they frequently lie upon the bare rock bottom, but there is often a kind of longitudinal timber laid underneath.

The tramroad is well laid and maintained; a man is employed for the purpose of effecting repairs. Rollers lie above the line as necessary, over which the hauling chain runs; these rollers are 2½ ft long and 6 in. diameter, and consist of a cast-iron cylinder with a wooden centre in which the wrought-iron pivot is fixed. As there are frequent small curves on the inclined gallery, also similar rollers are placed vertically at both sides of the line, as well as small guiding sheaves, 9 in. diameter and 4 in. wide, on the line itself, on which the chain runs.

The axles of the rollers are usually fixed to the sleepers.

A four-wheeled iron wagon, provided with a tipping arrangement, runs on this inclined tramway. The wheels are of cast-iron, 18 in. diameter and only ⅝ in. thick. A brass bush provided with four projections fits therein and is fixed by wooden wedges; the nave is only 2¾ in. long. The wagon contains nearly 22 cu. ft, 20 to 25 cwt of ore, and, including the wagon, the whole load may amount to 3,000 or 3,500 lb. The wagons are drawn by an iron chain, the links of which are 3½ in. long and ½ in. thick. The hauling is done by means of a waterwheel; the haulage is one-way. The wagons which are drawn upwards loaded must afterwards be let down again by their own weight; for this a brake arrangement is used. About 25 or 26 wagons with 20 cwt of ore are hauled in 24 hours; by day, when everything goes smoothly, 15 or 16 wagons can be hauled in 12 hours.

The weight of the heavy iron chain is disadvantageous to the haulage, because it is not balanced; also the chain links frequently break, causing damage and interruption to the haulage.

XIX. Inclined Plane on the Tavistock Canal

The Wheal Crebor copper mine lies 2 miles Engl. south of Tavistock, in Devonshire. The Tavistock Canal,[2] completed 9 years ago, which connects the Tavy with the Tamar, goes past this mine; as well as the Crowndale mine, which is 1 mile south of Tavistock, and where there is a coke oven and a tin-smelting furnace.

The Wheal Crebor Mining Company holds a very substantial interest in the canal company, amounting to 350 shares. The Duke of Bedford holds the remaining 50 shares of the total of 400 into which the capital of the company is divided. The canal is 2½ miles long above ground, in addition to a navigable length of 1½ miles Engl. underground. Near its union with the Tamar there

[1] *The German text gives* 2,400 *ft English.—Ed.*

[2] *The Tavistock Canal was incorporated by Act of* 27 *July* 1803 (43 *Geo. III, cap.* 130).—*Ed.*

is a self-acting plane 120 fathoms (105 fathoms Pruss.) long, and of 240½ ft Engl. vertical height, or a slope with an angle of 15⅝ degrees. There are two branches, the first of which is not far from Wheal Crebor and is 1½ miles long, leading to the slate quarry at Millhill. The second branch, on the other side of the main navigation, is only ¼ mile long. The canal is 16 ft Engl. broad at the upper surface and 9 ft at the bottom; the depth of water is 3½ ft. Where the canal goes underground through the hill, the entrance is 9 ft high and 6½ ft wide; it is built in elliptical brickwork. The brickwork section is not long, however, and the greater part of the tunnel consists of firm rock. The canal works were completed in 14 years, and cost £70,000. At present, the undertaking shows an annual profit of about £500, which amounts only to $\frac{5}{7}$ per cent of the working capital. The canal company maintains the canal and the connecting self-acting plane and machinery only; those who make use of the canal must provide all tackle themselves. For the use of the canal a ton (20 cwt) of limestone costs 6 pence (5 grs. 3 pfg.); tin and copper 18 pence (15 grs. 9 pfg.); and coal 20 pence (17 grs. 5 pfg.).

By reason of frequent grounding in the navigable stretch, the wooden boats are much damaged and require considerable repairs. With much advantage, boats made of iron plates riveted together have been introduced. The plates are barely ¼ in. thick; the boat is 30 ft long, 4½ ft wide, 2½ ft deep, and holds about 4½ tons (90 cwt) lading. The weight of the boat should amount to 1½ tons (30 cwt), an estimate, however, which is too small. The cost of building is £60 to £70 (420 to 490 thl.). The upper edge of the boat is framed with a bar 3 in. wide and ⅝ in. thick; the bottom is covered with wood; the steering rudder is made of iron plate; two wrought-iron crossbars serve to support the side walls of the boat. The content ofthe boat can be reckoned at about 300 cu. ft. The boat is loaded with five containers which weigh up to 200 lb; therefore up to 1,000 lb can be carried. With 12 in. in the water, the boat displaces about 120 cu. ft of water, amounting to 7,200 lb. The weight of the boat, therefore, would be 6,200 lb or nearly 3 tons.

That branch of the canal which extends from Wheal Crebor to the slate quarry at Millhill has to surmount a height of 19½ ft Engl. It would have been possible to do this by two locks, but the upper part of the canal has so little water that it might not have been possible to fill the locks. A cast-iron tramroad 156 fathoms (136 fathoms Pruss.), in length was built, therefore. It is 70½ in. wide and ascends 19½ ft, or 1½ in. per fathom (6 ft Engl.), or an angle of $1°.11'.37''$.

A wagon about 20 ft long moves on this tramroad, and can be let down so deep in the water that the boat can proceed on to it, whereupon boat, lading, and wagon, together about 8 tons, are brought from one part of the canal to the other by three horses. The empty boat is drawn upwards, and the laden one downwards, by one horse. The rails are 8 ft long, 3½ in. wide without the flange, and 1 in. thick; the flange is 1 in. high, 1 in. thick at the bottom, and ¼ in. thick at the top. Each rail has three oblong holes by which it is spiked to thick wooden sleepers laid 3 ft apart.

The 20 ft long wagon consists of a thick plank framework; the wheels are of cast-iron and 24 in. diameter, disc-shaped and only ¾ in. thick. The construction is similar to that employed for the wheels of the mine trams at the Wheal Crebor Mine, and arranged according to the same method as the mine trams at the previously-described Whingill Mine near Whitehaven.

The wheel nave is 6 in. long and has a closed bush at the front. On the back of the nave is a round plate with four tabs, and this is screwed to the nave by 4 small bolts. The wrought-iron axle is 2 in. diameter and passes through a 2¼ in. hole in the plate. The diameter of the bush is larger than this, namely 3 in. The end of the axle which fits into the wheel has a recess ¼ in. deep turned in it at 3 in. from the end; in this recess are placed two half-rings of brass or iron ¾ in. thick and 1¾ in. wide. The back plate is first put on the axle, then the half-rings, then the wheel is fitted on over them and the back plate fixed on. A small hole is made in the bush which is closed by a plug; this serves as a lubricating hole. As the wheels are closely fitted and all parts turned, they must run very well, and the lubricant can be retained for a long time.

In the slate quarry at Millhill, there is an inclined cast-iron tramroad upon which the wagons filled with slates are drawn upwards, and the empty wagons lowered, by a simple horse-gin. The gauge of the tramroad is 44 in. The rails are 3 in. wide without the flange and $\frac{7}{12}$ in. thick; the flange is $\frac{11}{12}$ in. high and $\frac{1}{2}$ in. thick. The wagons have cast-iron wheels 19 in. diameter, with a rim 1 in. wide, eight spokes, and a nave 7 in. long. The wagon body is wood and rests on a wood block; it is arranged to tip and turns on a horizontal axle. An iron hook secures it during the hauling; when this is disengaged, the body is allowed to tip and is unloaded easily.

Where the Tavistock Canal ends near Morwellham, it lies 240$\frac{1}{2}$ ft Engl. above the high water mark in the bed of the Tamar. The tide ascends as far as here from Plymouth, where it discharges into the sea.

From the canal, a self-acting plane 120 fathoms (720 ft Engl.) long descends to the river. By the river are many warehouses, a mill at which manganese-slag is ground, many coke ovens, and large sheds for copper ore. The last-named are so situated on the slope of the hill that a tramroad leads down to them from the self-acting plane and the ore from each mine can be tipped through tumbling holes into separate sheds. The self-acting plane has two parts, one of which leads to the level of the river; the other ends 30 ft above this point. Above, at the end of the canal, there is a waterwheel by which the empty wagons are drawn upwards. Each part can be worked separately. The waterwheel is simple and can work only in one direction. The two tracks of the tramroad are 35 in. from one another; the gauge is 46 in. The rails are 69 in. long, $\frac{3}{8}$ to $\frac{3}{4}$ in. thick, and 3$\frac{1}{2}$ to 4 in. wide including the flange; the flange is 2 in. high, $\frac{1}{2}$ in. to $\frac{7}{12}$ in. thick at the bottom, and $\frac{1}{4}$ in. to $\frac{1}{3}$ in. at the top. The rail is provided at each end with a hole $\frac{3}{4}$ in. square, and is fastened by spikes to wooden or stone sleepers. At very dirty places on the track near the River Tamar, and where the line crosses highroads, trough-shaped rails are laid. These are 34$\frac{1}{2}$ in. or 69 in. long; 3$\frac{1}{2}$ to 4 in. wide; 1$\frac{1}{12}$ to 1$\frac{1}{2}$ in. deep inside; $\frac{1}{2}$ in., $\frac{2}{3}$ in., or $\frac{3}{4}$ in. thick at the bottom; and 2$\frac{1}{4}$ to 2$\frac{3}{4}$ in. wide at the top.

The wagon is of sheet-iron strengthened by iron bars. It has unequal wheels, the front ones 15 in. diameter, the rear ones 18 in. diameter, and is arranged for tipping. It is drawn up and let down by an iron chain composed of links 4 to 4$\frac{1}{4}$ in. long, 2$\frac{1}{2}$ in. wide, and $\frac{1}{2}$ in. thick. The chain runs upon iron friction rollers lying in the middle of the track; these are hollow cylinders, 7$\frac{1}{2}$ in. diameter, 18 in. long, and are provided with rims projecting 1$\frac{1}{2}$ in. The rollers are fitted inside with wood through which passes a wrought-iron axle 25$\frac{1}{2}$ in. long. When the wagon comes over the end of the tramroad, an arrangement is employed by means of which the wagon itself puts the axle of the waterwheel out of gear with the chain-drum, so that the waterwheel continues to turn without moving the wagon further. The waterwheel is overshot, 28 ft high and 4 ft wide. It sets in motion a sloping shaft by means of bevel wheels, and this shaft, likewise by means of bevel wheels, turns the axle of the chain drum, which is 6 ft diameter and 2 ft wide, and the brake wheel for one part of the self-acting plane. From this shaft a similar shaft and drum for the other part of the plane can be moved by gear wheels; these shafts can be put in or out of gear by a simple arrangement.

A platform at the upper end of the self-acting plane is in the same slope as that plane. As soon as the wagon comes on this, its weight presses the platform down to a horizontal position. This platform is connected by an iron bar with a lever lying below it; this lever is connected by a pulling rod with another lever which supports, on its opposite arm, the trunnion bearing of the chain drum. Therefore, when the platform sinks, the trunnion bearing is elevated and puts the drum bevel wheel out of connection with the one on the sloping shaft from which the motion is derived. To facilitate this action, a counterweight pulls on the trunnion lever by means of a chain. In addition, there is an iron bar on the lever, provided with a handle so that the machine attendant can put either chain drum out of gear.

The brake consists of an upper and a lower cheek, which are drawn together simultaneously by a lever. This lever turns about an iron axle and is connected with the lower cheek by a chain, and with the upper cheek through an iron rod and a short lever, the end of which presses the upper cheek downwards when the rod moves upwards. At the opposite ends, the brake cheeks are connected by an iron bar which turns about a pivot in the lower cheek, and this pivot is supported by two iron rods which allow it a little freedom.

In front of every lode there is a large horizontal turnplate, to the level of which the platform is pressed by the weight of the wagon; from this the wagons are brought on to the tramroad, which in the immediate neighbourhood is provided with two sidings, and leads to the canal.

XX. Self-acting Plane from the Shropshire Canal to the Severn near Coalbrookdale

About 2 miles below Coalbrookdale, the Shropshire Canal is united with the Severn by a self-acting plane 793 ft long[1] and with a vertical drop of 207 ft, or an angle of 15⅛ degrees. The railway thereon is of cast-iron, built in the manner of a tramroad. The rails are the strongest and thickest of the kind that we have seen; also, they lie on longitudinal timbers 14 in. wide and thick, and these upon wooden cross-sleepers. The whole inclined plane is well paved. The tramroad has three lines of rails, so that it forms two tracks with one common rail; in the middle of the plane, where the full and empty wagons pass one another, there are four lines of rails forming two separate tracks. On one track the rail flanges are inside, and on the other track outside. The rails are 70 in. (6 ft Engl.) long; 7 in. wide, exclusive of the 2½ in. high and 1 in. thick flange; and 2 in. thick. On one end there is a projecting point 5 in. broad and 1½ in. long and on the other end a suitable notch in which the point fits. In addition, there is a tab on the flange through which a wooden plug is inserted to connect the two rails; four 1-in. square holes enable the rails to be spiked to the longitudinal timbers.

The connection of the rails by wooden plugs is seldom used, and only a few rails are provided with the small recess in the middle of the flange. In the track are iron rollers over which the rope runs.

The canal boats which arrive on the Shropshire Canal are let down on this self-acting plane. A wooden wagon frame is used for lowering them. Most of the canal boats are of wood, 18 ft long, 5 ft 2 in. wide, and 2½ ft deep, in the clear. One such boat weighs about 1½ tons empty, and the greatest load amounts to about 5 tons, whereby it still has about 3 in. freeboard. The cargo consists of coal and iron.

The wooden frame on which the boats are placed is of very simple construction. On the two outer frame beams stand posts 5 ft high, fixed by struts, and connected at the top by an iron cramp provided with three eyes for the attachment of the chain. The frame has two large front wheels 27 in. diameter, and two small hind wheels 16 in. diameter, which have an inside gauge of 43 in. They are 6 in. wide at the rim, and 10 in. long in the nave; these lie wholly under the frame. Outside of the wagon there are also two outer flanged wheels of 24 in. diameter on the same axle as the small hind wheels, and with a gauge of 78 in. When the wagon is drawn out of the canal upon the bank of the self-acting plane, these wheels run upon a special railway, and thereby enable it to pass over the highest point of the bank without rubbing. The weight of the wagon frame is . . 2 tons

and the boat with its load . . . . 6½ tons

therefore the total weight is . . . . 8½ tons

or 170 cwt. About 100 boats can be let down in 12 hours.

A 16-in. steam-engine stands on the highest point of the self-acting plane, on the ridge formed by it and by the short inclined plane leading to the canal. This serves to draw the wagon with the canal boat out of the upper part of the canal. It also completes the drawing up of the wagon coming up the self-acting plane, when the full wagon, with the boat, has plunged into the water, and thus so

[1] *The authors point out later that Thomas Tredgold gives this length as* 1,050 *ft in his book, 'A Practical Treatise on Rail Roads and Carriages', which was first published in* 1825.*—Ed.*

reduced its effective weight that it is no longer able to draw the empty wagon right to the top of the plane.

On the axle of the steam-engine there is a small gear-wheel with 24 teeth, which engages with a larger wheel with 96 teeth, on the axle of which is fitted the rope drum of 7 ft diameter, with the brake wheels for the self-acting plane. The small gear-wheel can be put in or out of gear by a contrivance operated in the engine house, so that the engine and the rope drum can move independently of one another. The rope goes from this drum over iron rope-sheaves 6 ft diameter and 5 in. wide, and then under the drum away to the self-acting plane; the rope-sheaves hang perpendicularly over the upper part of the canal, so that the wagon can be drawn forward over the ridge.

A pinion with 40 teeth on the axle of the steam engine engages with a wheel with 96 teeth mounted on an intermediate axle which also carries a pinion with 28 teeth. This intermediate axle has a bearing-seat inside the engine house, and can be put in or out of gear by means of a lever, so that this axle can be put in motion or at rest according to choice. The pinion of 28 teeth engages with a wheel of 80 teeth which is mounted on the axle of a small chain-drum and brake wheel; through this drum, and a chain, the canal boat is drawn out of the upper part of the canal on to the top of the self-acting plane. The manipulation of the brake is as follows:—As soon as the full wagon comes to the bottom, the laden boat is removed by a workman and pushed into the canal, and, in exchange, an empty boat is brought on and affixed. The full down-going boat does not draw up the empty one the whole distance, because the tramroad goes entirely under the surface in the lower canal, and the loaded boat, as soon as it plunges into the water, loses much of its weight. As soon as the empty boat stops, a workman releases the brake on the large rope drum, while another puts the engine in connection with this drum and sets it in motion so that the boat shall continue its journey upwards and across the ridge of the self-acting plane. When the boat has reached the ridge it goes slowly on the tramroad into the upper canal. The large rope-drum is then disconnected from the engine, the engine stopped, and two workmen push the empty boat off the wagon, put on a full one instead, and attach the wagon to the chain of the small drum. This chain was unwound during the time that the empty boat was passing over the ridge, at which time also the chain-drum was connected with the engine. As soon as the full boat is pushed on, the engine is started, and, by means of the chain, draws the full boat upwards out of the canal on to the ridge of the self-acting plane. One workman stands at the engine, the other at the brake. As soon as the boat is across, it is attached to the rope of the large drum and let down the plane by means of the brake. To permit this, the engine is stopped, and the chain-drum disconnected from it; this done, the workman removes the chain from the wagon, and puts on the brake, keeping it on until the full boat plunges into the water at the lower canal. In between, a workman has time to attend to the firing of the engine, and to bring the boats into position and attach them, so that little time is lost. The workman at the lower canal is also employed in the unloading, etc., as affixing and detaching the boats requires little time. At Coalport on the lower canal a ton of coal costs 8*s*. (2 thl. 24 grs., or 16 grs. 9 pfg. per ton Pruss. of 4 bushels), a very low price when the fact that already the coal has come from the pit many miles distant is taken into consideration.

All the connecting wheels of the brake-arrangements are cast in two parts, which reduces the danger of breakage when they are being staked on their axles. The axles are of cast-iron 4 in. square, the journals $3\frac{1}{2}$ in. diameter, the wheels 3 in. in the split part. The engine crank is 18 in. long. The rope which lets down the wagons is $3\frac{1}{2}$ in. diameter.

The large rope-drum makes $\frac{1}{4}$ of a revolution for one revolution of the engine shaft, and the small chain-drum makes $\frac{7}{48}$ or about $\frac{1}{7}$ of a revolution. Tredgold, in his book: *A Practical Treatise on Rail Roads and Carriages* gives the length of this incline as 1,050 ft. In addition, he states that the Shropshire Canal has two other self-acting planes; the second 1,800 ft long and with 126 ft fall, or an angle of somewhat over 4 degrees; the third 1,050 ft long and with 120 ft fall, or an angle of $7\frac{1}{6}$ degrees.

XXI. Slipway for hauling a ship out of the water for repairs

In the harbour of Whitehaven there is a contrivance on Morton's principle for hauling sea-going ships on to the land for repairs, and for putting them back into the sea. This arrangement consists of a winding apparatus and an iron railway. The latter comprises three lines of rails lying 20 ft distant from one another; the frame which goes on them has four low wheels of suitable width and provided with flanges. The rails are flat on top and have a wider under seat; the whole foundation consists of solid masonry. The middle rail is channel-shaped, and in its base is a toothed bar; the wheels run upon 4 to 5 in. thick rims; the railway is 200 to 300 yards long and has a slope of about 5 in.; and goes so deep below flood level that ships of 150 to 200 tons lading can lie on it. The separate rails are 5 ft long and are fastened to the stone sleepers by spikes and wooden plugs. The hauling apparatus consists of two cranked axles whereon different wheels of 20, 24, and 30 in. diameter can be fitted, any of which acts upon the next axle lying in front. From this the power is transmitted to a second axle, and from that to the load axle; on the last-named there is a toothed wheel having four large teeth which engage in the links of a chain by which the ship is wound to the top. The first gear wheels stand in such a relation that the power of 32 men working the winch handles is multiplied 65 times, $81\frac{1}{4}$ times, or $97\frac{1}{2}$ times, according to which wheel is put on the cranked axle. The chain is forced, by two wheels lying in front of the chainwheel, to surround somewhat more than half the circumference of the latter; one of these leads the chain to the wheel from the ship carriage, while the other guides the chain to a drum on which it is wound by means of a special winch, completely separate from the remaining hauling winch, so that the free part of the chain shall not be in the way. In this manner the hauling chain always operates in one direction and at one leverage.

The chief part of the arrangement, however, is the frame upon which the ship is placed, drawn to the top, repaired, and lowered back again. This frame is built of thick oak timber, strengthened by iron plates, and runs upon the railway. Its length is adjusted according to the length of the ship to be repaired, which rests with its keel upon the frame in such a manner that a good part of the frame remains free in front of and behind the ship. The frame runs upon strong cast-iron wheels of about 9 to 12 in. diameter on the railway already described; the wheels are spaced about 6 ft apart. Wooden blocks are loosely laid on the middle part of the frame and are fixed only by light iron clamps; the keel of the ship rests on these blocks. Wooden beams are laid on the frame at suitable distances, and upon these lean the side props which support the ship on both sides and prevent it from tipping over. A cast-iron pawl engages with the teeth of the middle rail, to prevent the frame and ship from sliding downwards; six or more of these pawls are employed according to necessity. These pawls are disengaged by crowbars when the ship is to be lowered.

The hauling apparatus, which is fixed on a strong iron frame at the upper end of the railway, is not used for lowering the ship.

D. PALMER'S, OR RAILWAY WITH ONE RAIL (MONORAIL)

The railways heretofore described all consist of two bars, so that the wagons that run on them have two wheels on each axle, one of which runs on each rail. To facilitate laying out a railway with reduced friction, and to make it independent of the small unevennesses of the ground, Mr Palmer has proposed and built a kind of railway which consists of a single bar, and the wagons have only one wheel on each axle. The track is erected on posts or columns at a suitable height above the ground, and the load hangs so far below the wheels that the wagon frame cannot overturn.[1] This railway has the disadvantage that its construction is not solid, or it becomes very expensive; that it can compensate only for very small unevenness of the ground; that the motive power can operate only with an inclined pull; and that special precautions must be taken for unloading and loading the wagons. Therefore, the scheme has not come into general use. Excepting the two now to be mentioned, no railways of this kind appear to have been built in England.

XXII. Palmer Railway in the Victualling Office at Deptford near London

This railway leads from the Thames across the yard of the Victualling Office up to the warehouse, and serves to transport provisions out of the warehouse to the ships, or the reverse. The railway consists of cast-iron columns which project from 3 to 5 ft out of the ground; these are provided with fork-shaped seats at the top and are spaced 10 ft apart. Planks 9 in. high and 3 in. thick rest in the forks on double wooden wedges, so that they can be set at the correct level very easily. On the upper edge of these planks, wrought-iron bars are spiked, which are $3\frac{1}{2}$ in. wide, somewhat convex, and $\frac{1}{2}$ in. thick in the middle. The ends of these bars are not square, but cut in a broken line, and rest, not directly on the plank, but on a small iron plate let into the wood.

The line is nearly horizontal, and has a fall of only about 20 minutes of angle to the river.

The wagons which run on this line have three wheels of 18 in. diameter, one behind the other; they have two flanges and the groove is shaped to fit the rail. These wheels are fixed to a wrought-iron frame which consists of three stirrups going over the wheels with connecting pieces below. The stirrups reach 2 or 3 ft below the railway, and are provided on both sides with an inclined platform, on which are placed the casks to be conveyed. For loading the wagons, there are two sloping frames at the same height as the wagon platforms, and between which the wagon has just room to pass. A wagon is loaded with 10 casks which weigh about $4\frac{1}{2}$ cwt each, therefore totalling 45 cwt. The wagon can be taken at 5 cwt, so that the whole weight comes to 50 cwt, which can be moved up the line easily by four men.

XXIII. Palmer Railway from the Limekilns and Brickworks at Cheshunt to the Lee Canal

From the lime and brick kilns at Cheshunt, in Hertfordshire, about 20 miles north of London, which lie on a main road, a Palmer railway leads to the Lee Canal in the flat and level Lee valley. The railway has a fall of 5 to 10 minutes of angle towards the canal; it is $\frac{3}{4}$ mile Engl. (580 fathoms Pruss.) long and serves to transport lime and bricks. The line rests on wooden posts which project on average $3\frac{1}{2}$ ft out of the ground; towards the limekiln, however, the bottom of the line is in a cutting in the ground, so that the posts stand in a kind of dry trench, the base of which is 9 ft wide. The wooden posts stand 10 ft apart, are 4 in. thick, and $7\frac{1}{2}$ in. wide; the top is fork-shaped 3 in. wide and cut 16 in. deep. In the bottom of this fork lies a block 12 to 15 in. long, in different heights, which is supported by a pair of inserted angle-pieces 14 in. high and 2 in. thick. Two wedges 2 ft long rest on this block with their inclined faces lying against one another, so that a horizontal support is always afforded to the plank which lies thereon. The planks are $10\frac{1}{4}$ in. high and 3 in. thick; they are 30 ft long and always meet in the middle of a post. Iron bolts with screws go through the post to hold together its fork-shaped end. There are oblong holes in the planks through which these bolts pass, so that the underlying wedges can be adjusted when necessary. On top of the planks a wrought-iron convex rail is laid, 4 in. wide, $\frac{1}{4}$ in. thick at the edges, and $\frac{1}{2}$ in. thick in the middle.

[1] *This refers to a device patented by Henry Robinson Palmer* (1795–1844) *on* 22 *November* 1821 (*Patent No.* 4618). *The line in the Royal Victualling Yard, Deptford, appears to have been brought into use in the latter part of* 1824. *The Cheshunt line was opened with considerable ceremony on* 25 *June* 1825. *Palmer was the moving spirit in the formation of the Institution of Civil Engineers, which had its origin in a meeting that he addressed on* 2 *January* 1818.—*Ed.*

The rails are 20 ft long with their ends cut obliquely, and they are fixed by no more than two or three spikes of ½ in. diameter with their heads countersunk in the rails. The rails have some spare holes which are used when one or other of the spikes breaks.

Some posts are made of three parts fixed together. The pieces are 6 in. wide; the middle piece is 3 in. thick, the side pieces are 2¼ in. thick, and they are bound together by three screw-bolts; the wedges lie upon screwed-in blocks which are 1 ft long at the top. Although these planks are very thick, they have become bent at some places because of the great distance between the posts and are propped up by pillars set under them subsequently.

There is a siding on the railway in the vicinity of the canal. Here the line is made double for a length of about 30 ft, and between the double piece and the single track there is a strong door 10 ft wide which is hinged to the single rail and may be fastened to either of the two tracks. The railway lies on the upper edge of the door. Directly over the hinge is a small turning piece of rail by which the severe angle which the door makes with the main railway is reduced. This railway passes over an ordinary road by a similar door.

The wagons on this railway have only two cast-iron wheels, 26 in. diameter, with two flanges; they are 5¼ in. wide including the flanges, which are ½ in. thick and project 1¼ in. They have six spokes and a nave 6 in. long and 2 in. wide. The wheel turns with a hollow cast-iron axle 2 in. thick and 12½ in. long, which lies in round brass bushes at both ends; these have an inside diameter of 1⅝ in., an outside diameter of 2½ in., and are 3⅜ in. long inside. They are fitted to seats on the wrought-iron stirrups which form the main frame of the wagon. Through the hollow cast-iron axle and the brass bushes is a wrought-iron axial bar 26 in. long, and 1 in. thick, the ends of which are fastened to the stirrup. This makes a firmer connection with the wagon frame. The two wheel centres are 46 in. apart. The platforms on which the wagon bodies are placed are 40 in. below the axle centres and are 17 in. apart. There is one wagon body on each side of the wagon, and each holds 20 cu. ft. One such body is laden with 20 cwt of lime or bricks, and therefore a wagon takes 40 cwt. One horse draws two such wagons or 80 cwt, exclusive of the bodies and the wagon.

On a disused standing wagon, there is a special arrangement for reducing the friction of the wheels on the axles, which is neither properly devised according to theory nor well carried out practically. The brass bushes wherein the cast-iron axle turns have a circular-segment-shaped slot, ¾ in. wide, cut in the upper part, and in this notch rests a 4 in. high iron friction wheel, on which the whole load of the wagon bears, while the brass bush is not entirely held fast in the wagon frame.

GENERAL REMARKS ABOUT RAILWAYS IN ENGLAND

The foregoing records what we found occasion to notice in the course of a journey to observe the railways in England. The different varieties are well explained therein by at least one example. This fulfils the object of the intention, namely: to note the use of the terrain and the surmounting of its difficulties; the manner of the arrangement of the line itself; the wagons employed thereon; and the motive power and other stationary machinery arrangements connected with it. The variety of execution is as great as that of the objects in view; a great contrast is provided by the difference between the light railways of wrought-iron at the Cornish copper and tin mines for the transport of ore, often of only inconsiderable length, to the larger railway of the same material from Bishop Auckland to Darlington and Stockton which opens up an entire coal region, establishes a new market, and will influence the whole coal trade to the sea. The distinction is not less important between the railway which uses the gentle descent of the valley, or else in level regions follows the natural contour of the ground, and those which send the greatest loads with incredible speed over high hill-ridges by using engines which together possess more than 100 horsepower. If these railways are diverse, nevertheless, their principal arrangement may be reduced to three kinds: English or *Railroads*; German or *Tramroads*;[1] and Palmer's railways, or those which have only one rail. Of the last-named, few have been made. The first, the English railways, are built partly of cast-iron and partly of wrought-iron; the second, German tramroads, are of cast-iron only; and the last, the Palmer's railways, are only of timber and wrought-iron. The wrought-iron English rails are considered to be the most satisfactory of all these kinds. Although these have not yet been employed often for larger plans, yet the outstandingly successful construction of the Darlington Railway has demonstrated clearly that they are suitable and useful for the largest plans, and for the still larger Liverpool & Manchester Railway only these have been considered. If these rails in larger and stronger form are suitable for larger schemes, so indeed there is no more suitable material than similar rails made on smaller dimensions for light railways which are not needed very long in one place, or for temporary purposes. On this account they are very important for mines, and are worthy of recommendation for the German mines. These rails are simple, easy to lay, durable, need little repair, and, where rolled from iron made by the puddling process, are cheap to produce. On this account, the German railways (*Tramroads*) are considered generally inferior to the English railways (*Railroads*). In a large part of England, in the south and midlands, tramroads predominate; only in the north of England do railways preponderate. The Palmer railways do not appear to afford the necessary security, nor to permit the use of the forms of wagon often necessary, so that they have not come into general favour.

The effect of the motive power, and the method of its employment, is dealt with in the descriptions of the individual railways, so far as we were able to observe. Trials on this subject, as well as many other interesting points about railway arrangements which invite remark, have been described by Wood, Viewer of the Killingworth Colliery, near Newcastle, and are given in a special work: *On Railroads*, London, 1825.

[1] English railways (*railroads, edge rails*) on which the wheels of the wagons have flanges; German railways (*tramroads, tram or flat rails*) in which the wheel rims are plain. (*Footnote by Authors.*)

STRENGTH OF THE RAILS

The bearing power of the rails is a most important point in connection with the laying of the larger railways, but it is one about which very few trials have been made hitherto. Wood has determined only the bearing power of cast-iron rails such as those employed on the Hetton and Dartmoor railways, and of wrought-iron rails as laid on the Darlington Railway.

The usual form of the English rails (*edge rails* for flanged wheels) is that of a parabolic curve on the underside. For the particular purpose when the weight rolls along the upper surface, the variable cross-section to produce the greatest strength is not yet determined accurately. When a bar is supported at both ends and is loaded at the middle, with the upper side straight, it is considered to be strongest when the underside consists of two half-parabolas; when, however, the bar is equally loaded at all points, which case comes nearest to that of the rolling load, then the bar is strongest when the underside is formed as a half ellipse.

The cast-iron rails, by the great stiffness of this form, bend hardly at all before they break, and on this account it is almost impossible to employ them in long pieces. If the difficulty of manufacture be ignored, then long pieces must be supported in the middle at suitable distances. These supporting points are not employed with cast-iron rails, however, as even a small sinking of the sleeper would be followed by the breakage of the rail. It is a great advantage of the wrought-iron rails that they can be employed in greater lengths. In Tredgold's opinion,[1] the parts between the intermediate supporting points possess considerably greater strength than separate pieces of equal length. The difference ought to go so far that, when the ends of the rail were perfectly fixed, the intermediate pieces should possess double the strength of separate pieces. Much may be said against an opinion which is not confirmed by experiment. Even now the basis on which Tredgold considers that one overall uniform height of rail is more suitable than the curved underside, for equal strength at every point, seems to be not entirely sufficient. The same writer declares that the stiffness in the first is greater than in the latter, and therefore it is more difficult to produce a bend in it. If the opinion of Tredgold for cast-iron rails merits little consideration, the same for wrought-iron is of greater importance, as with this the condition arises that the manufacture of the under curve is not only beset with difficulties, but it also destroys the inner cohesion-condition of the iron in working, and places restrictions on the length of the intermediate parts.

The authors then reproduce in abbreviated form Wood's table of 'Experiments on the Strength of Cast-Iron Rails' and comment:—

Wood does not give a close specification of the iron employed in these tests, but it should be noted that generally at the English iron foundries three different sorts of pig-iron are supplied for the casting trade marked Nos. 1, 2, and 3, of which the first sort is a gray, soft, and tough iron; the second is a mottled iron; and the third is a white, hard iron.

The remainder of the work consists of lengthy extracts from the First (1825) *Edition of 'A Practical Treatise on Rail-Roads, and Interior Communication in General' by Nicholas Wood, dealing with motive power and other trials, with some quotations from the First* (1825) *Edition of 'A Practical Treatise on Rail Roads and Carriages' by Thomas Tredgold. As these works are available in the original English, it is thought unnecessary to include here a translation from the German of material which the authors themselves translated from known English sources.*

[1] 'A Practical Treatise on Railroads and Carriages.' London 1825. (*Footnote by Authors.*)

INDEX

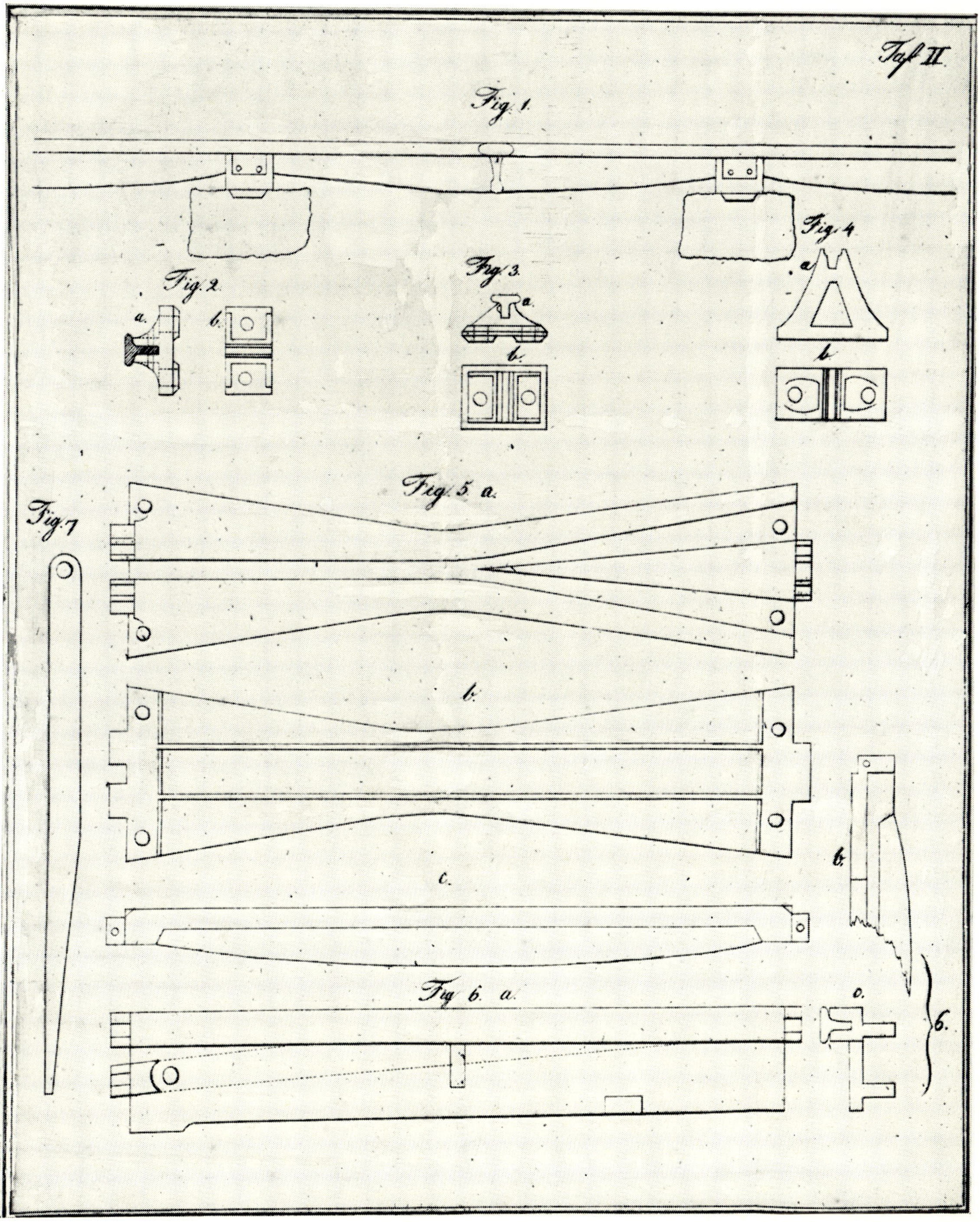

PLATE I. Figs. 1–7.

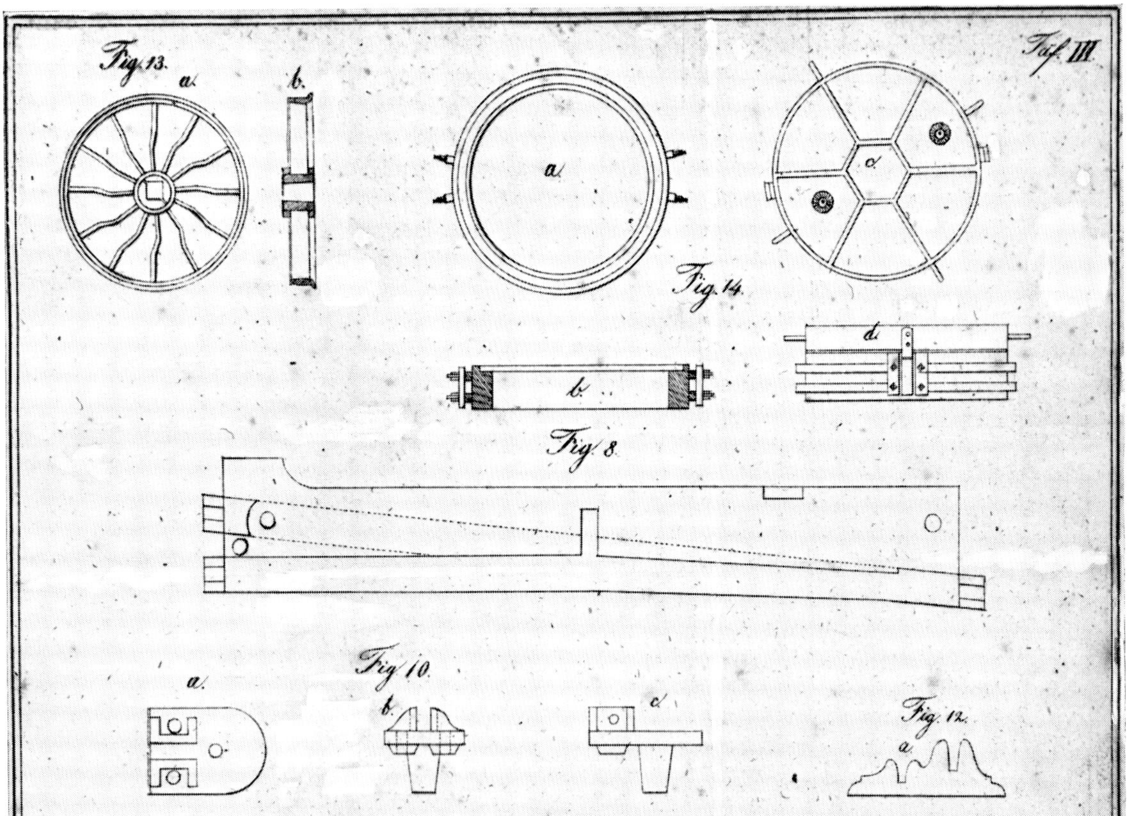

PLATE II. Figs. 8–14. Maasstab für Fig. 13 u. 14 (Scale of figures 13 and 14). Fuss (Feet).

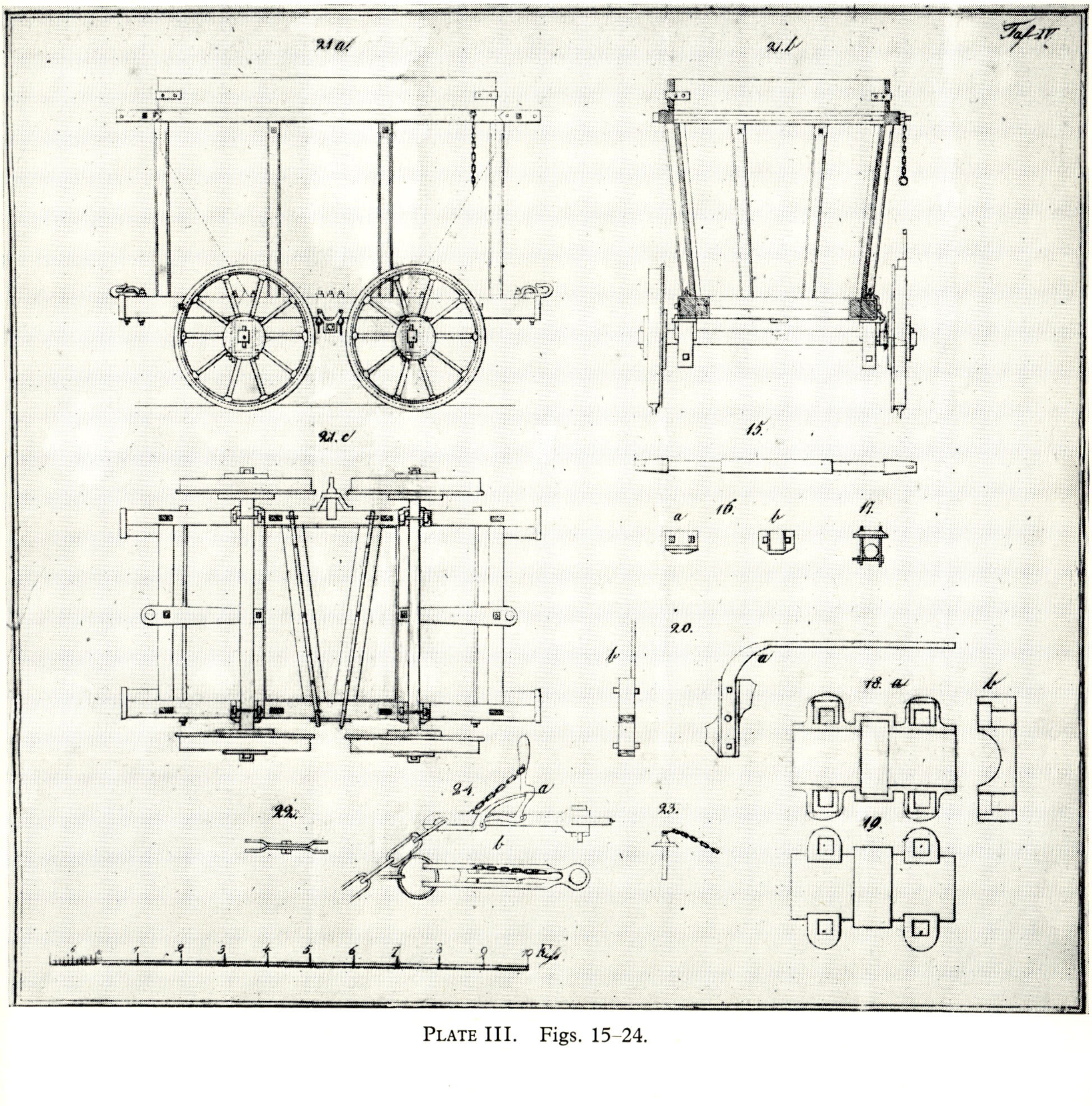

PLATE III. Figs. 15–24.

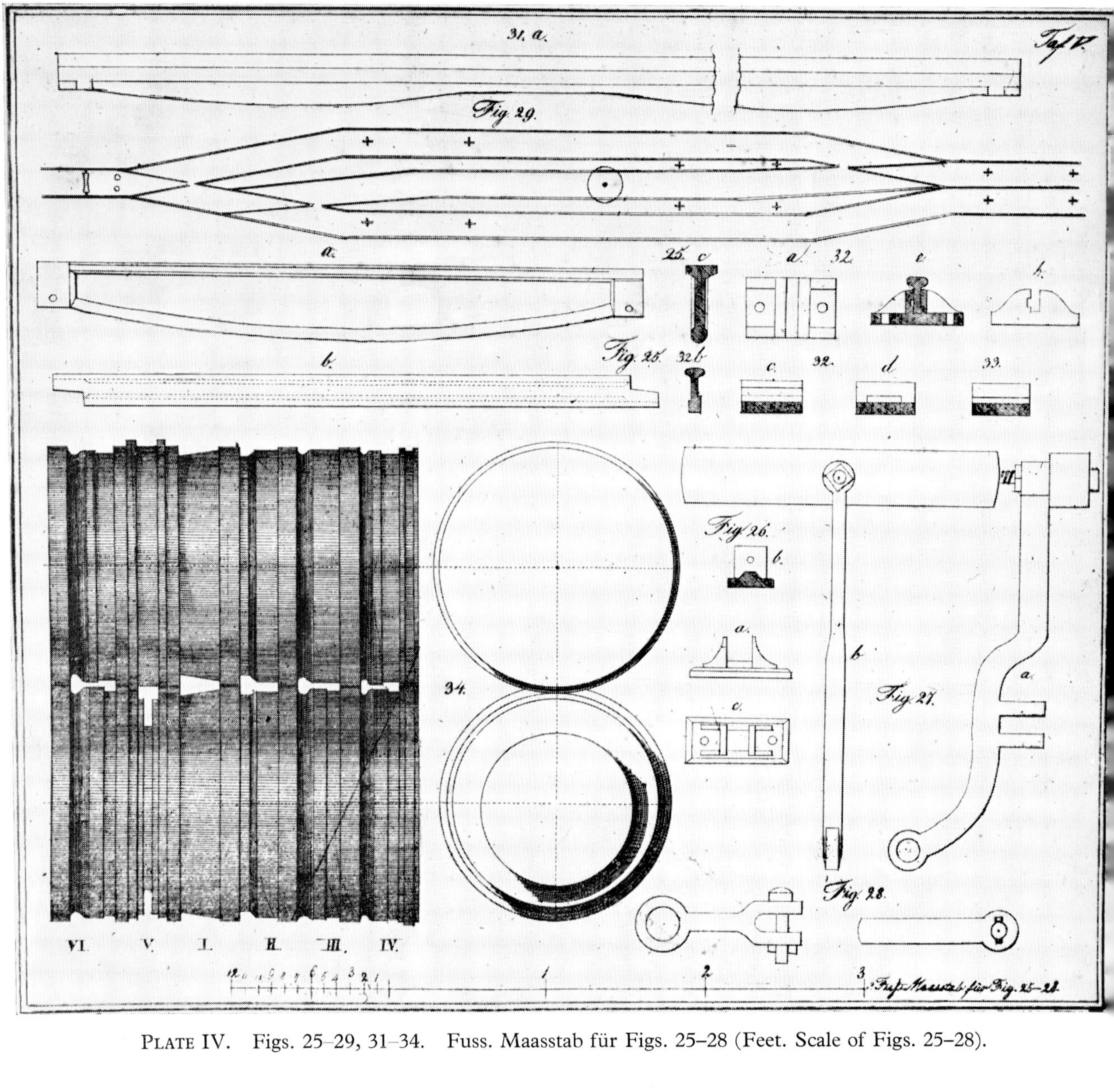

PLATE IV. Figs. 25–29, 31–34. Fuss. Maasstab für Figs. 25–28 (Feet. Scale of Figs. 25–28).

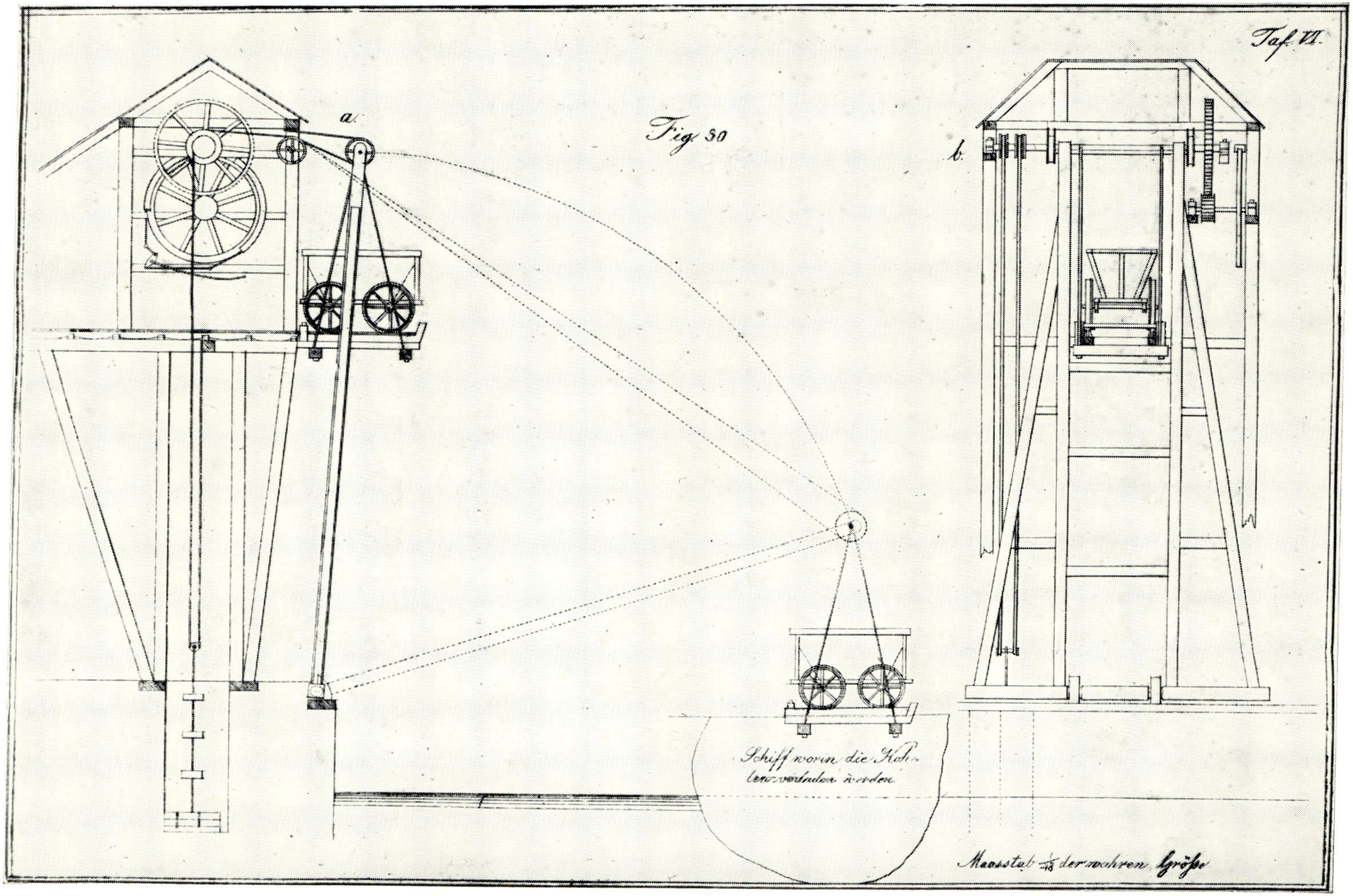

PLATE V. Fig. 30. Schiff worin die Kohlen verladen werden (Ship in which the coal is loaded). Maasstab 1/48der wahren Grösse (Scale 1/48 of the true size). The present reproduction, however, is somewhat smaller than the German original.

Brant x